MANNERS MADE EASY

A WORKBOOK FOR STUDENT, PARENT, AND TEACHER

WRITTEN BY

JUNE HINES MOORE

ILLUSTRATED BY

JIM OSBORN

BROADMAN
&HOLMAN
PUBLISHERS

Nashville, Tennessee

To my husband Homer and our beloved family:
Gregory, Jeffrey, Leslie, Laura Elizabeth, and Mary Catherine.

All student pages are removable and reproducible.

Unless otherwise noted, Scripture quotations have been taken from the Holman Christian
Standard Bible, copyright © 1999, 2000 by Holman Bible Publishers. Used by permission.

Text copyright © 2001 by June Hines Moore

Illustration copyright © 2001 by Jim Osborn

Cover: Valerie Simmons/Masterfile

Published in 2001 by Broadman & Holman Publishers
Nashville, Tennessee

A catalog record for this book is available from the Library of Congress

8 9 10   07 06 05 04

Manners Made Easy

A Word from the Author

Teacher Pages

Student Pages

A Word from the Author

The parent or teacher who accepts the challenge of inspiring students to learn proper behavior, interpersonal skills, and good manners will be rewarded for their efforts. I believe that good manners were God's idea first. My overall goal in writing this workbook/teacher's guide is to enable parents and teachers to motivate their students to learn, and more importantly, to practice good manners, gain self-confidence, and try never to embarrass another person or themselves.

After they have completed this workbook, it is my hope that shy students will turn self-consciousness into confidence based on the person they are in Christ – created in His image to be His representatives. Bold students, who may think highly of themselves, should recognize their dependence on God and develop a desire to think of others first.

These lessons are designed to help students become more self-confident and considerate. They will also encourage students to practice the Golden Rule, which is *Just as you want others to do for you, do the same for them* (Luke 6:31).

Ideally, *Manners Made Easy* will be taught in six consecutive weekly sessions, as set forth in this workbook. If a seventh week is needed, additional discussion material is included. To aid the parent/teacher, this book is divided into two sections. The student pages are perforated so they can be removed and duplicated. All quizzes (with answers) have been repeated in the teacher pages.

Teacher's First Challenge

The teacher's first challenge will be to properly motivate students to learn and practice the guidelines laid out in these exercises. There is a distinction between motivating and manipulating someone. To motivate is to offer something someone wants, while to manipulate is to get someone to do something for another reason, such as avoiding punishment.

There is an old adage that says *You can lead a horse to water, but you cannot make him drink.* However, as someone else wisely stated, if you put salt in his oats, he will gladly drink. Your job as the teacher is to create or uncover a desire in the students to want to learn good manners. The incentives, or the salt, may include making friends or being well-liked. For example, older students may be thinking of the responsibility that comes with driving a car, dating, going out with friends, or interviewing for a part-time job. The following are some ways to bring out the "salt" needed to motivate students.

- Get students involved in ways that appeal to their different learning styles.
- Give students specific responsibilities with clear instructions for individual or team activities.
- Show enthusiasm! The student's interest is closely linked to the teacher's enthusiasm and passion to learn.
- Show relevance. When they understand the reason or the application for what they are expected to know, students are more likely to learn and remember.

The first challenge of motivating students may not be easy. However, using proper motivation and effective tools should make the learning process easier for students.

Teacher's Second Challenge

The teacher's second challenge is to incorporate a variety of teaching methods into their teaching methodology, because not all students learn the same way.

Some of the basic approaches to learning that educators have identified are:

• Students who like to listen to and talk about what they're studying

• Students who need visual aids

• Students who want to interact with what is presented to them

• Students who like to reason through difficult problems

• Students who want to consider the relevance of the material as it relates to their own strengths and weaknesses

• Students who learn best as they work with others in teams to accomplish a task

Most students learn in a combination of these approaches. Activities such as role-playing, working in teams, personalizing lessons, watching demonstrations, performing hands-on tasks, brainstorming, and taking quizzes should make your job easier.

Teacher's Third Challenge

The last challenge is to help students never to use their newfound knowledge to embarrass, criticize, or belittle someone who does not know the rules of proper behavior. Many of the rules of etiquette are based on common sense and good reason. It is important to teach students not to judge those who have had no opportunity to learn and practice good manners.

As a parent and teacher, my favorite verse to claim is "Now we pray to God that you do nothing wrong, not that we may appear to pass the test, but that you may do what is right." (II Corinthians 13:7)

June Hines Moore

Note: Good manners are for everyone. If the teacher of this workbook is not permitted to use biblical references, the etiquette rules may be taught without using the Bible lessons. The student pages are reproducible for use in the home or church school classroom. In addition, page 46 of the teacher's section can be reproduced to be distributed to each student.

MANNERS
Made Easy

Lesson One
WHO NEEDS MANNERS ANYWAY?

LESSON OVERVIEW	SUPPLIES NEEDED
This lesson has four main topics: • What manners are all about • Where manners came from • Why we need manners today • What manners can do for us as individuals	• Two or three styrofoam balls • Toothpicks

ABOUT THIS LESSON

Students today do not always have the opportunity to learn proper manners. They live in a world where there is a growing pattern of rage and rudeness. Young people see adults behaving rudely on the telephone, driving thoughtlessly while using a cell phone, failing to introduce people, and ignoring common courtesies such as saying 'please' and 'thank you.'

When you begin teaching a class, try to compliment the students on the good manners they have. Sometimes you must make an effort to look for some courtesies to mention, such as saying 'please,' and 'thank you,' or opening doors for others.

In the first lesson we will talk about what manners are all about, where they came from, why we need them, and what they can do for us. Begin by having the students write their name at the top of the first page of their lesson.

What Manners Are All About
Discuss the first student page of Lesson One with the students.
"Manners are the happy way of doing things." Ralph Waldo Emerson

OBJECT LESSON - *What do you know about porcupines? Tell the following story which is based on a German fable.*

Porcupines are small rodents covered with sharp, hollow quills and coarse hair. Their protruding quills poke anything that comes near them, even one another. Imagine a group of porcupines trying to huddle together in freezing temperatures. They are cold when they are by themselves and poke each other when they try to get close to stay warm. Finally, they discover that if they work together, they can keep warm without poking each other. Having consideration for others shows that we care. That's what manners are all about.

ACTIVITY

With the styrofoam balls containing toothpicks, demonstrate how the porcupines worked together. Explain by working together they were able to get closer to each other, protecting themselves from freezing temperatures, thereby making life more comfortable.

You may ask students if they can think of similar human experiences that demonstrate the principle of good manners.

Q&A

Manners are words and actions that show we (care) about others. Good manners help us make (friends) and develop good social skills. Good manners make us and others feel happy and comfortable.

1. Were you born knowing good manners? (no)
2. How do you get good manners? (learn them)
3. Who needs to learn good manners? (everyone)

ETIQUETTE: *Our Ticket to Success*

The word etiquette means a set of manners that have reasons. It is pronounced etta-kut. These rules help us know how to behave properly. The word *etiquette* is a French word that means *ticket*. In the days of the French kings, the lords and nobles were given "etiquettes" to tell them to stay off the grass when they were not inside the Versailles Palace where Louis XIV held court sessions. Other tickets were given to them to show where they were to stand in court, representing their province (state).

We should keep rules of etiquette in our head, just like math or grammar rules. We keep manners in our hearts to prevent us from embarrassing others or ourselves.

ACTIVITY

Make sure each student can say etta-kut and not etta-quet.

LESSON

An etiquette teacher went to an executive's office to discuss an upcoming seminar for his employees. As she entered his office, he said, "We really need a lot of etta-quet taught around here." Why do you think she could not correct him? Because in this instance it would have embarrassed him and would have been rude. So as they talked she used the word etta-kut instead of the word manners and before she left his office, he was saying etta-kut. As a result of saying the word correctly, she was able to teach him the correct pronunciation without embarrassing him.

MANNERS
Made Easy

TEACHING TIP - To help students understand the difference between etta-kut and etta-quet you may tell about a similar experience or adapt this story into your own circumstances. The main point is to instill in students that by knowing the rules of etiquette, we can avoid embarrassing ourselves. Keeping manners in our heart will prevent us from embarrassing others. This premise should be repeated throughout the workbook study.

RULES OF ETIQUETTE (MANNERS) HAVE REASONS

Rules exist in nearly everything we do. Rules of etiquette exist in sports to show fairness and safety. Even our courts and legislative sessions have strict rules of etiquette. On television, we see that a man is called "the gentleman from (his state)" and a woman is called "the gentle lady from (her state)."

Sometimes the rules of etiquette evolved from specific actions. The story goes that we shake hands in our country because in the early days, men carried guns to defend themselves as they moved westward. When they approached someone, they extended their empty hand in a vertical position to show they were not drawing their gun. Our handshake evolved from this early gesture.

In other countries it is appropriate for men to kiss each other on the cheek. In Asian countries people bow to each other.

Q&A

What have you observed about other cultures greeting one another?

For the remainder of this lesson, students can work individually, in teams, or in a brainstorming session listing actions they consider to be good manners. Select someone to make a permanent chart, poster, or list on the board. This list will represent some good manners the students already know and some they will learn from one another.

LESSON ONE QUIZ

1. How do we get manners? (**learn them**)
2. What does learning good manners do for us? (**gives us confidence, makes us feel good about ourselves, or makes others feel good**)
3. What is the oldest rule of good manners? (**Golden Rule**)
4. What can we learn from the fable of the porcupines? (**cooperation, teamwork, consideration**)
5. Name at least one of the categories of good manners. (**Acts of Kindness, Dining Manners, Customs**)
6. Do all countries have the same customs that we do? (**No**)
7. Practicing good manners keeps us from doing what? (**Embarrassing ourselves or others**)
8. Why is it rude to correct the manners of others? (**It can embarrass them**)
9. What should you do instead of correcting someone? (**Set a good example, demonstrate proper behavior**)

MANNERS
Made Easy

LESSON ONE BIBLE STUDY

KEY SCRIPTURE REFERENCES:

And Jesus increased in wisdom and stature, and in favor with God and with people. (Luke 2:52)

Just as you want others to do for you, do the same for them. (Luke 6:31)

BIBLE LESSON:

The Bible tells us the Trinity is made up of God, the Father; Jesus, God's son who became flesh; and the Holy Spirit.

Jesus, God's son, was born to earthly parents, Mary and Joseph. Jesus' birth was a miracle because Mary was still a virgin. Because He was born to earthly parents, Jesus was completely God, yet completely human.

Luke 2:52 says *Jesus grew in wisdom and stature.* Jesus grew in all the same physical ways that you and I do. In addition to growing physically, Jesus grew in knowledge, in His relationship with His family and friends, and He also grew closer to God.

Jesus also had to learn the customs and laws of His day.

Other things Jesus probably learned were to play fairly at games, set the table, conduct Himself at the Temple, be a well-behaved guest, greet people who came into Joseph's carpenter shop, and other types of interaction which required the use of good manners.

Just as Jesus learned and practiced the principle for using good manners, He also taught this principle to others in Luke 6:31. He told the people around Him that they should treat others just as they would like to be treated. Today we call this the Golden Rule.

BIBLE QUIZ

1. Who originated the idea of good manners? (**God**)
2. What is the name of the rule good manners are based on? (**The Golden Rule**)
3. What does Luke 6:31 say? (**Just as you want others to do for you, do the same for them**)
4. What verse tells us that Jesus grew physically, spiritually, and mentally? (**Luke 2:52**)
5. Write Luke 2:52 here: (**And Jesus increased in wisdom and stature, and in favor with God and with people.**)

Lesson Two
HOW TO INTRODUCE MYSELF

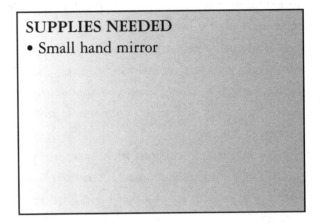

LESSON OVERVIEW
This lesson has three main topics:
- Why we feel uncomfortable around people we do not know
- Learn and practice the Six S's
- Learn and practice a proper handshake

SUPPLIES NEEDED
- Small hand mirror

ABOUT THIS LESSON

Students who know how to introduce themselves to others are more comfortable and more confident than students who are unsure of themselves in group situations. When students know how to properly meet and greet people, they make a better first impression. We all get only one chance to make a first impression.

When students are away from their family and friends, they need to know how to interact with new people. When students make a good first impression they usually represent themselves and their families in a positive way.

In this lesson, students will learn the formula for introducing themselves and meeting others. This formula, called the Six S's, will equip them with tools they can use the rest of their lives.

Begin this lesson by letting students brainstorm possible answers to the following questions which are found on their lesson sheets. Let them fill in the blanks, then discuss their answers.

Q&A

How do you feel when you are the new one in a group and you don't know anyone? Why do you think no one introduced you or included you in the conversation?

Remind students the good manners they learn in this lesson will show them how to approach the new person, tell him or her their name, ask what his or her name is, and ask that person to join their group.

Where are some places this might happen?

Tell students that after this lesson they will be prepared to introduce themselves comfortably. They will learn and practice the Six S's, beginning with the handshake. The Six S's will be a tool they can use the rest of their life to make a good first impression.

LEARNING THE PROPER HANDSHAKE

Handshakes should be firm, not wimpy. Males and females shake hands the same way. A proper handshake begins by extending your right hand in a vertical position with the thumb pointing upward and your fingers together. Allow the web between your thumb and index finger to meet the web of the other person's hand while gripping firmly. An exception to this rule is if someone extends a crippled or arthritic hand. Then you should shake the hand gently, but still using your whole hand. No finger shaking.

On very formal occasions such as wedding receptions, men should wait for the woman to extend her hand first. However, in business situations and at other times, it does not matter who extends the hand first. Do not pump someone's hand up and down. Shake hands long enough to exchange greetings. Either person may release the handshake first. To express special affection, you may place your left hand on top of the handshake. If the other person extends his or her left hand, take it with your right hand. The other person should turn their hand so your palms are together.

Review the rules of the proper handshake listed on their student page and answer any questions.

You can demonstrate the proper handshake by having one student come to the front and shake hands with you. Each student should practice how to hold the right hand for a proper handshake, how to execute a right-to-left handshake, and a gentle handshake.

LEARNING THE SIX S'S

1. **Stand.** You should stand when you meet someone for the first time. You should also stand to greet someone if that person is standing. Both men and women should stand, however women do not need to rise from a table (such as a conference or dinner table) unless the newcomer is an older or more distinguished individual.
   After you stand, S's 2, 3, 4, and 5 are performed almost simultaneously, but not hurriedly.
2. **Smile.** It takes only 14 muscles to smile but over 70 to frown. A smile is the same in any language. Have students take their small hand mirrors out and watch themselves smile and then frown. Tell them to say "Hello! How are you?" as they smile, and the same words as they frown. Ask if they hear the difference in the friendly tone of voice versus the flat tone.
3. **See their eyes.** Look people in the eye when meeting or talking to them. To avoid staring, look from their mouth to their eyes. If you feel uncomfortable looking people in the eye, practice at home with a mirror. You may feel silly at first, but if you can introduce yourself before a mirror, you will become more comfortable doing so in public.
4. **Shake their hand.** Use the proper handshake practiced in the previous section.
5. **Say your name.** Say "Hello! My name is _____."
6. **Say their name back to them.**

Q&A

Why do you think it is important to say someone's name back to him or her as learned in Step 6?

Let students give their answers, then reinforce the following points:
• It helps you to remember that person's name;
• It makes the other person feel good to hear you say their name;
• It gives you a chance to make sure you understood the name correctly. If not, the other person can use this opportunity to tell you their name again.

The use of first and last names will be explained in a subsequent lesson. For now, let the students use their first and last names in #5 when introducing themselves. Then for #6 they may respond using the other student's first name only.

Omit #5 if you are simply greeting an old friend. Instead use #6. For example, "Hello, John."

ACTIVITY

Assign a partner to each student. If there is an odd number of students, one student may be assigned an additional partner. Ask two students to volunteer to come to the front of the room and go through the Six S's together. If necessary, offer gentle critiques.

While learning to perform the Six S's, have students follow the script on page 12. Later they can add words they are comfortable with, such as 'Hi' instead of the more formal 'Hello.'

The following is one version of an appropriate dialogue. The teacher and students may be more creative with their responses to a greeting as long as they practice all six S's.

Both of the students will stand, smile, see each other's eyes, and extend their right hand.

The first student says, "Hello, my name is _____." He or she extends their right hand and shakes their partner's hand properly.

The second student says, "Hello, _____. I'm _____. It's nice to meet you." The first student says, "It's nice to meet you, too, _____."

After completing the Six S's, the students may make a statement or ask a question which relates to their circumstances. A neutral statement might be "I have just moved here. I like it so far." Neutral questions might be "Have you been here long?" or "Have you known the host a long time?"

Hello, my name is Wes.

Hello, Wes. I'm Glenna. It's nice to meet you.

MANNERS
Made Easy

LESSON TWO QUIZ

1. What are the Six S's? **(Stand, Smile, See their eyes, Shake hands, Say your name, Say the other person's name by saying, "Hello, Mrs. Smith.")**

2. Have you practiced using the six S's outside the classroom? When?

3. Which of the Six S's is the most difficult to remember? **(Number 6.)**

4. What are three reasons #6 is so important? Student answers should include the following:
   a) **Saying it helps us remember the name**
   b) **It makes the other person feel good**
   c) **Repeating it permits us to make sure we understood it correctly**

5. Now that you know the Six S's, will you be more confident in going up to new people in your church or neighborhood to introduce yourself and make them feel welcome? If not, which of the S's do you feel you need to work on?

6. Why do we shake hands in our country? **(It is our patriotic custom.)**

7. What did you learn with the mirror? **(A smile is always better than a frown. That smiling makes a difference in the way I look and in the way I sound.)**

LESSON TWO BIBLE STUDY

Key Scripture Reference:

Then said his sister to Pharaoh's daughter, Shall I go and call to thee a nurse of the Hebrew women, that she may nurse the child for thee? (Exodus 2:7 KJV)

ADDITIONAL SCRIPTURE REFERENCES:

Genesis 24, Exodus 1:22-2:10; John 3:1-5, John 4:5-26

BIBLE LESSON

For many years the Hebrew people were held captive in Egypt by Pharaoh. Even while they were slaves they continued to grow in strength and number. Pharaoh, who had heard about their mighty God, was afraid they would overtake his rule. So he ordered all the male Hebrew babies be thrown in the river.

However, there was one Hebrew mother who made a basket of reeds, covered it with tar, and hid her baby in the Nile River.

One day the Pharaoh's daughter came to the river to bathe. When she discovered the baby in the basket, she immediately had compassion on him. Miriam, who had been watching from the bushes, ran to Pharaoh's daughter and offered to find a Hebrew mother to raise the baby.

Of course, the customs were very different in those days, but we can assume that Miriam introduced herself to Pharaoh's daughter before daring to ask about the baby. Miriam was a servant and she showed a great deal of bravery stepping forward to speak to Pharaoh's daughter.

Before giving the baby back to his own mother to raise, Pharaoh's daughter named him Moses, which means *to bring out of the water.*

Miriam's obedience showed she trusted God. Her courage in introducing herself to the princess earned her a place in God's history because Moses would become a great leader who would guide God's people out of Egyptian bondage.

BIBLE QUIZ

1. Who was the little girl who was brave enough to introduce herself to the Pharaoh's daughter? **(Miriam)**
2. Read the additional Scripture references and list others who introduced themselves. **(Nicodemus to Jesus, Jesus to the woman at the well, and Eliazer to Rebecca.)**
3. How did Miriam's courage and actions make a difference in the history of God's people? **(She played a part in history by saving her brother Moses, who led the people of Israel out of Egypt and into the promised land.)**

Lesson Three
HOW TO INTRODUCE OTHERS

LESSON OVERVIEW

This lesson has four main topics:
- Making introductions
- Greetings
- Making conversation after being introduced
- Remembering names

SUPPLIES NEEDED
- Crown or hat

ABOUT THIS LESSON

Making a smooth introduction of others is not always easy, even for adults. If students learn the basic rules and how to practice them, they will develop a social awareness that will open doors, win friends, and help them feel good about themselves.

Trying to make an introduction is the most important element of the introduction. The rules will become easier with practice. This lesson will help students introduce others correctly, know who to introduce first, know which person to introduce to whom, know how to remember the names of those they are introducing, and know what to do if they cannot remember a name.

HOW TO INTRODUCE OTHERS

Remind students they learned how to introduce themselves in lesson two. In this lesson they will learn how to introduce adults and friends to one another. The most important rule about introductions is to try. If they can't remember everyone's name, try anyway. Think of it as giving someone a present. When they give names to people who do not know one another, they make them feel more comfortable. Always begin the introduction using the most honored person's name first.

Here are the rules which clarify who is the most honored person.

1. Introduce the younger person to the older person (honored).
2. Introduce a male to a female (honored).
3. Introduce the less-distinguished person to the more distinguished person (honored).
4. Give first and last names if you can.

Turn first toward the person in the "honored" position. Address this person as
  "Grandmother, Reverend, Brother Smith, Mr. or Mrs. Jones."
  Example: Say "Grandmother, this is my friend from school, Laura Andrews."
  (Always say the last name.) Turn to Laura and say, "Laura, this is my Grandmother,
  Mrs. Jenson."
  Most people have more than one grandmother, so her last name may be different
  from yours. Also, Laura would feel uncomfortable calling your grandmother,
  "Grandmother or Grandma."

  A good rule to remember when introducing people is never to use nicknames.
  Remind students to give each person's name to the other. He or she can then say hello
  and call the person by name. Example: Let's say your grandmother's name is Grandma
  Jenson. Everyone else will say, "Hello, Mrs. Jenson."

Example: Introducing your mother or father to your friend's parent (honored).

  Give your parent's last name if it is different from yours. Start with the honored person and simply say, "I'd like to introduce _____ to you."

Example: Introducing your sibling to your friend (honored).

  "Johnny, this is my sister, Amy." or "Amy, this is my brother, Johnny."

Example: Introducing your parent to your teacher (honored):

  "Mrs. Hodges, I would like to introduce my mom, Jane Brown (or Mrs. Brown)." Your teacher may prefer to call your mom Mrs. or Ms. Brown, although they are both adults.

  Review with students how to determine the most honored person. The honored position is based on age, gender, or position such as a governor, minister, teacher, etc. In addition, we usually give the honored designation to persons outside of our family.
  Sometimes an introduction is based on one's judgement concerning who should get the most respect under the circumstance of the introduction.
  Ask the students to draw a crown over the most honored person in each of the examples listed on their student page. When they finish you can ask students to volunteer to identify the individuals they crowned.

GREETINGS

Review the five S's, explaining why the sixth S is not used after someone gives their name to another person in an introduction.

Review the following examples for greeting someone.

Greeting someone after they have been introduced to you

"Hello, it is nice to meet you, Mrs. Jenson." (Always say the person's name.)

Your response as you walk away from someone you have just met

"It was nice to meet you, Mrs. Jenson." (Use the person's name.)

Always greet adults with a title such as Mr., Mrs., Miss, or Dr.

Sometimes when people are very close but are not relatives, parents permit their children to use an adult's first name. Other times adults have such long, difficult last names that students are permitted to use a title and the adult's first name such as Ms. Shannon (Waberloskivev).

Greeting someone you already know

Simply say hello or hi along with their name and then make conversation. Example: "Hi, Mary, how are things going with you?"

Greeting someone you already know but have not seen for a while

It is never polite or considerate to greet someone with "Hi, remember me?" Always give your name if you have not seen the person for a while. Think about how uncomfortable you would feel if you had to say, "No, I do not remember you."

If you have no help from the person who introduced you, ask a nice question, such as "Where do you go to school?" or make a statement about how you know the one who introduced you. Example: "John and I go to the same church".

What happens if you are with a group of people you know, and a friend walks up who does not know the group?

If the group is four or fewer people, you can name each person in the group to the friend, but if the group is large simply say your friend's name and let the others introduce themselves. Example: "This is my new neighbor, Hank McGrew." Someone in the group should use the six S's: "Hi Hank. I am Kerry Heath." Then the others should follow.

REMEMBERING NAMES

Do you ever have trouble remembering names? Everyone has trouble remembering them sometimes. What should you do if you forget someone's name and you need to introduce him or her to others? Ask students to check one of the three choices listed on their student pages. Remind students that they must always make the effort to introduce people – even people they think may already know one another. Pretending to forget an introduction is not acceptable.

Check one: _____ Make up a name and hope no one notices.

                    _____ Skip the introduction.

                    __(X)__ Say, "I'm sorry, but I can't remember your name."

REVIEW THESE POINTS:

• If you don't understand the name when you are introduced to someone, say "I didn't quite get your name" or "Could you repeat your name, please?"
• If someone mispronounces your name, politely correct them. Example: Your name is Jean but you are introduced as Jane. After the introduction, simply say "It's Jean."

LET'S PRACTICE

Have students write the introduction of a close friend to the teacher, then have them read or perform it.

Before practicing these examples, have the students draw a crown over the honored person in each example. The honored person is listed in parenthesis.

1. Introduce your classmate and your father. "Dad, this is Jimmy Ramsey. He plays on my soccer team. Jimmy, this is my dad, Sam Jones." (**father**)
2. Introduce your mother and your classmate's mother. "Mrs. Ramsey, this is my mom, Sara Jones. Mom, this is Mrs. Ramsey, Jimmy's mom." (**classmate's mother**)
3. Introduce a male classmate and a female classmate. "Laura, this is Jimmy Ramsey from my soccer team. Jimmy, this is Laura from my fifth-period class." (**female classmate**)
4. Introduce your father and your minister. "Reverend Carpenter, I would like to introduce my dad, Sam Jones. Dad, this is Rev. Carpenter, our new minister of youth." (**minister**)

MANNERS
Made Easy

THE SIMPLEST INTRODUCTIONS ARE AS FOLLOWS:

"Mrs. Hodges, this is my friend Kayly Combs."

Mrs. Hodges says, "Hello Kayly. I'm glad to meet you."

Kayly says, "Hello, Mrs. Hodges. It's nice meeting you."

Note: Students may use the phrases: "This is" or "I would like to introduce". After they learn the proper way to make introductions, they can shorten the process by looking at the honored person and giving the other person's name and something about him or her. Then turning to the less honored person, the introducer (a student in this case) gives the name and information about the honored person. For instance, "Rev. Carpenter, my dad, Sam Jones. Dad, Rev. Carpenter, our new youth minister."

Note: For very young students you may decide to teach only the simplest introduction such as: "Mrs. Hodges, I want to introduce my friend Kayly Combs to you" or "Mrs. Hodges, this is Kayly Combs."

Mrs. Hodges says "Hello, Kayly. I'm glad to meet you."

Kayly says, "Hello, Mrs. Hodges. It's nice meeting you."

CONVERSATION AFTER THE INTRODUCTION

Ask students why it is more important to introduce each person by more than just their name. Go over the following paragraph from the student page.

Often it is difficult to know what to say or do after we have been introduced, said hello, and said the new acquaintance's name. The person making the introduction should tell you something about the other person, such as their relationship. Example: "This is my friend; my mom; my teacher." You may also tell how the introducer knows the individual or why the introducer wants you to meet the other person.

Possible answers for fill-in-the-blank examples: "Have you known Sara long?" "Have you been here long?" "I just moved here." The students may have other ones.

Points to remember in making conversation:
1. In a group, always try to include everyone in the conversation. Do not talk to only one person.
2. Listen and try not to interrupt.
3. Do not say something that might hurt someone's feelings.

ROLE PLAYING

Ask two volunteers to come to the front of the class to be introduced – one girl and one boy.

Ask the class who the honored person is – the girl or the boy.

Place the crown on the girl's head.

The teacher will need to introduce the boy to the girl. Walk the student through the proper way to make an introduction, using the Six S's and the proper handshake.

Ask one of the students to introduce the other one to you, the teacher.

Ask the class who the honored person is.

The introducer will place the crown on the teacher's head. Continue practicing different situations. If necessary, make a dialogue sheet for students to follow. Remind students that the introducer needs to give some kind of information about each person in the introduction. Giving some additional information allows the two strangers to have something to talk about after the introduction.

If possible, have each student in the classroom come to the front to practice an introduction.

LESSON THREE QUIZ

1. What is the most important rule about making introductions? (**Trying**)
2. What should you do if you cannot remember someone's name? (**Ask politely or say something like "I can't seem to remember your name. You will have to help me out."**)
3. Who wears the crown in any introduction? (**The most distinguished/honored person.**)
4. What three factors determine who wears the crown? (**Age, gender, and position**)
5. Why is it necessary to give the first and last name of a person? (**So that they can call each other Mr. or Mrs. using their last name.**)
6. In a group, always try to include (**everyone**) in the conversation.
7. When talking with others, always listen and try not to (**interrupt.**)
8. Do not say something that might (**hurt someone's feelings.**)

 # LESSON THREE BIBLE STUDY

KEY SCRIPTURE REFERENCE:

And he brought Simon to Jesus. When Jesus saw him, He said, "You are Simon, son of John. You will be called Cephas" (which means "Rock"). (John 1:42)

ADDITIONAL SCRIPTURE REFERENCE:

John 1:40-42

BIBLE LESSON:

John 1:40-42 is the story of two brothers, Andrew and Simon (Peter), who were fishermen. Andrew had heard Jesus speak and was so moved by Jesus' message, he wanted his brother Simon to meet Jesus. Andrew is mentioned only a few times in Scripture, but notice what an important thing he did. He brought his brother to meet the Lord Jesus. Jesus would later give Simon the name Peter, which means *rock*. Peter became one of Jesus' greatest followers. After Peter met Jesus, his goals and priorities changed. He was changed by Jesus' love and spent his life communicating that love to others.

Like Andrew, we must take seriously our responsibility to introduce people to each other. We never know how important that introduction might be.

BIBLE QUIZ

1. Why did Andrew want to introduce his brother to Jesus? (**He had met Jesus and heard Him speak. He believed in Jesus and wanted his brother to meet Him too.**)
2. Who would have been the most honored person when Andrew introduced his brother to Jesus? (**Jesus, because of His position.**)
3. Write a possible introduction Andrew might have used. (**Lord Jesus, I want to introduce my brother Simon to you. Simon, this is Jesus Christ, my Savior and Lord.**)
4. Did God have a plan for Peter's life? (**Yes**) Explain your answer. (**Peter became one of Jesus' disciples and one of His most faithful followers.**)

Lesson Four

TELEPHONE MANNERS

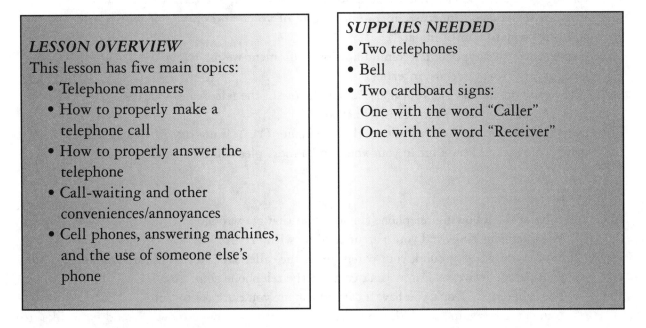

LESSON OVERVIEW

This lesson has five main topics:

- Telephone manners
- How to properly make a telephone call
- How to properly answer the telephone
- Call-waiting and other conveniences/annoyances
- Cell phones, answering machines, and the use of someone else's phone

SUPPLIES NEEDED

- Two telephones
- Bell
- Two cardboard signs:
  One with the word "Caller"
  One with the word "Receiver"

ABOUT THIS LESSON

Children and adults alike usually delight in talking on the telephone. But often they begin using the phone before they have learned the rules of proper telephone etiquette. Yet, with good training, anyone can make a good impression on the phone.

Alexander Graham Bell invented the telephone in 1876. Until that time the fastest form of communication had been the telegraph, which was based on a set of number/sound signals. Today the telephone has become an instant form of communication. In addition, it is a life-saving tool that connects us to the world around us. Since the first telephone which had a crank handle on the side, the telecommunication industry has experienced rapid growth. Today, we live in what is called the *information age*. We deal with voice mail, car phones, cordless telephones, beepers, and answering machines. There is little doubt that students need to learn and begin using good telecommunication manners early.

We all talk on the telephone and we all make an impression – a good one or a bad one. When communicating over the telephone our voice and choice of words are the only tools we have to use. We either sound cold, unfriendly, and rude, or we sound warm, friendly, and alert.

MANNERS
Made Easy

Q&A

1. Can you name some adjectives to describe the impressions we often make while talking on the telephone? (**Bored, friendly, disinterested, excited, happy, sad**)
2. Why are telephone manners so important? (**Tone of voice and choice of words are our only way to communicate.**)
3. Name some other types of telecommunication equipment we use today. (**Beepers, two-way radios, internet**)
4. What rules do you have at your house about the use of the telephone? (**Varies**)
5. To whom do you make phone calls? (**Varies**)
6. Do you think you can hear a smile on the telephone? (**Yes**) If not, try it with a class-mate. You should hear a lift in your voice and a more pleasing tone when smiling.

ACTIVITY

Mark the parts of the following telephone conversation that are wrong.

_____ 1. The telephone rings and your parent answers with "Hello."
__X__ 2. From a noisy background, your parent hears the caller say "Hey, is Danny around?"
_____ 3. Your parent answers: "Danny can't come to the telephone right now."
__X__ 4. The caller says, "Don't you have a cordless phone you can take to him?"
_____ 5. Your parent again says, "Danny can't talk on the phone now. Would you like to leave a message?"
__X__ 6. The caller says, "No!" Then your parent hears a loud click followed by a dial tone.

Now you will learn how to properly make a telephone call and how to avoid being rude on the phone.

HOW TO PROPERLY MAKE A TELEPHONE CALL

Here are the rules for the proper way to make a telephone call. The rules spell out TIME.

    T ake the **Time** of day into consideration.
    I dentify yourself and ask to speak to your friend.
    M ake sure your friend can talk at this time.
    E nd the conversation if you made the call by saying good-bye first.

Example: You are calling your friend Paul after school. (**T**) His mom answers the phone. If you recognize her voice, say, "Hello, Mrs. Randall. This is Joey. May I speak to Paul?" If you do not recognize the voice, say, "Hello, this is Joey. May I speak to Paul?" (**I**) When he comes to the phone, make sure to ask if this is a good time to talk. Say, "Can you talk now?" (**M**) End the conversation by saying good-bye first, because you made the call. (**E**) Remember that someone else may need to use the phone at your house or your friend's house.

Lesson One
WHO NEEDS MANNERS ANYWAY?

"Manners are the happy way of doing things."
Ralph Waldo Emerson

Manners are words and actions that show we _____ about others. Good manners help

us make _____ and develop good social skills. Good manners make us and others feel

happy and comfortable.

HOW DO WE GET MANNERS?

Were you born knowing good manners? _____

How do you get good manners? _____

Who needs to learn good manners? _____

Etiquette: Our Ticket to Success

Manners are sometimes called etiquette, a French word. It is pronounced etta-kut. The rules of etiquette help us know how to behave properly. The word *etiquette* is a French word that means *ticket*. In the days of the French kings, the lords and nobles were given "etiquettes" to tell them to stay off the grass when they were not inside the Versailles Palace where Louis XIV held court sessions. Other tickets were given to them to show where they were to stand in court, representing their province (state).

We should keep rules of etiquette in our head just like math or grammar rules. We keep manners in our hearts to prevent us from embarrassing others or ourselves.

MANNERS
Made Easy

RULES OF ETIQUETTE (MANNERS) HAVE REASONS

In our country, shaking hands is a customary gesture used in greeting others. Customs in other countries include bowing or a kiss on the cheek. The rules of manners in our country are based primarily on the following categories. Make your own list below. Some expressions of good manners may fit under one or more than one column. Think of as many as you can.

ACTS OF KINDNESS	DINING MANNERS	CUSTOMS
Saying, "I'm sorry."	Eating with your mouth closed	Shaking hands when greeting someone
Opening doors for people	Using your napkin	Pledging allegiance to the flag

Lesson One Quiz

1. How do we get manners? _____

_____

2. What does learning good manners do for us?_____

_____

3. What is the oldest rule of good manners?_____

_____

4. What can we learn from the fable of the porcupines?_____

_____

5. Name at least one of the categories of good manners._____

_____

6. Do all countries have the same customs that we do?_____

7. Practicing good manners keeps us from doing what?_____

_____

8. Why is it rude to correct the manners of others?_____

_____

9. What should you do instead of correcting someone?_____

_____

MANNERS
Made Easy

 ## LESSON ONE BIBLE STUDY

KEY SCRIPTURE REFERENCES:

And Jesus increased in wisdom and stature, and in favor with God and with people. (Luke 2:52)

Just as you want others to do for you, do the same for them. (Luke 6:31)

BIBLE LESSON:

The Bible tells us the Trinity is made up of God, the Father; Jesus, God's son who became flesh; and the Holy Spirit.

Jesus, God's son, was born to earthly parents, Mary and Joseph. Jesus' birth was a miracle because Mary was still a virgin. Because He was born to earthly parents, Jesus was completely God, yet completely human.

Luke 2:52 says *Jesus grew in wisdom and stature.* Jesus grew in all the same physical ways that you and I do. In addition to growing physically, Jesus grew in knowledge, in His relationship with His family and friends, and He also grew closer to God.

Jesus also had to learn the customs and laws of His day.

Other things Jesus probably learned were to play fairly at games, set the table, conduct Himself at the Temple, be a well-behaved guest, greet people who came into Joseph's carpenter shop, and other types of interaction which required the use of good manners.

Just as Jesus learned and practiced the principle for using good manners, He also taught this principle to others in Luke 6:31. He told the people around Him that they should treat others just as they would like to be treated. Today we call this the Golden Rule.

BIBLE QUIZ

1. Who originated the idea of good manners? _____

2. What is the name of the rule good manners are based on? _____

3. What does Luke 6:31 say? _____

   _____

4. What verse tells us that Jesus grew physically, spiritually, and mentally? _____

5. Write Luke 2:52 here: _____

   _____

Lesson Two
HOW TO INTRODUCE MYSELF

How do you feel when you are the new one in a group and you don't know anyone?

_____

Why do you think no one introduced you or included you in the conversation?

_____

_____

People who have good manners should introduce new people to their friends, but often the people in the group you want to enter do not know how.

If you are already part of a group and see someone who is alone, the good manners you learn today will show you how to go over to a new person, tell him or her your name, ask what his or her name is, and ask that person to join your group.

Where are some places this might happen?_____

_____

If no one introduces you, you may introduce yourself. Afterwards, if the people in the group know how to use good manners, they will say hello and then give you their names, then you will say hello to them using their name.

Now you will learn and practice the Six S's, beginning with the handshake.

MANNERS
Made Easy

LEARNING THE PROPER HANDSHAKE

Handshakes should be firm, not wimpy. Males and females shake hands the same way.

Extend your right hand in a vertical position with the thumb pointing upward and your fingers together. Allow the web between your thumb and index finger to meet the web of the other person's hand.

Follow these rules when shaking hands with someone:
• Shake hands until each person has said a greeting.
• Do not pump someone's hand up and down dramatically. Two or three shakes will do nicely.
• Either person may end the handshake.
• On formal occasions, the gentleman waits for the lady to extend her hand.
• In business situations, it does not matter who extends their hand first.

LEARNING THE SIX S's

What are the six steps for properly meeting and greeting someone new?

1. S_____   2. S_____   3. S_____

4. S_____   5. S_____   6. S_____

Which one of the six steps would you omit if you are simply greeting someone you already know and are not introducing yourself for the first time?

_____

Before you practice the six S's, let's talk about the "smile."

Why is the smile so important? _____

Does a smile make a difference when we talk to someone? _____

Get out your hand mirrors and smile and then frown. Which is more pleasing? _____

PRACTICE

After the teacher assigns you to a partner, stand, smile, see each other's eyes, and extend your right hand.

The first student says, "Hello, my name is _____." He or she extends their right hand and shakes their partner's hand using the proper handshake.

The second student says, "Hello, _____. I'm _____. It's nice to meet you."

The first student says, "It's nice to meet you, too, _____."

After completing the Six S's, you may want to ask a question which relates to your circumstances. A neutral statement might be "I have just moved here. I like it so far." Neutral questions might be "Have you been here long?" or "Have you known the host a long time?"

MANNERS
Made Easy

LESSON TWO QUIZ

1. What are the Six S's? 1. S_____   2. S_____

                                       3. S_____   4. S_____

                                       5. S_____   6. S_____

2. Have you practiced using the six S's outside the classroom? When?

_____

3. Which one of the Six S's is the most difficult to remember?

_____

4. What are three reasons #6 is so important?

_____

_____

5. Now that you know the Six S's, will you be more confident in going up to new people in

your church or neighborhood to introduce yourself and make them feel welcome?

_____

If not, which of the S's do you feel you need to work on? _____

6. Why do we shake hands in our country? _____

_____

7. What did you learn with the mirror? _____

_____

 # LESSON TWO BIBLE STUDY

KEY SCRIPTURE REFERENCE:

Then said his sister to Pharaoh's daughter, Shall I go and call to thee a nurse of the Hebrew women, that she may nurse the child for thee? (Exodus 2:7 KJV)

ADDITIONAL SCRIPTURE REFERENCES:
Genesis 24, Exodus 1:22-2:10; John 3:1-5, John 4:5-26

BIBLE LESSON:

For many years the Hebrew people were held captive in Egypt by Pharaoh. Even while they were slaves they continued to grow in strength and number. Pharaoh, who had heard about their mighty God, was afraid they would overtake his rule. So he ordered all the male Hebrew babies be thrown in the river.

However, there was one Hebrew mother who made a basket of reeds, covered it with tar, and hid her baby in the Nile River.

One day the Pharaoh's daughter came to the river to bathe. When she discovered the baby in the basket, she immediately had compassion on him. Miriam, who had been watching from the bushes, ran to Pharaoh's daughter and offered to find a Hebrew mother to raise the baby.

Of course, the customs were very different in those days, but we can assume that Miriam introduced herself to Pharaoh's daughter before daring to ask about the baby. Miriam was a servant and she showed a great deal of bravery stepping forward to speak to Pharaoh's daughter.

Before giving the baby back to his own mother to raise, Pharaoh's daughter named him Moses, which means *to bring out of the water*.

Miriam's obedience showed she trusted God. Her courage in introducing herself to the princess earned her a place in God's history because Moses would become a great leader who would guide God's people out of Egyptian bondage.

BIBLE QUIZ

1. Who was the little girl who was brave enough to introduce herself to the Pharaoh's

   daughter? _____

2. Read the additional Scripture references and list others who introduced themselves.

   _____

3. How did Miriam's courage and actions make a difference in the history of God's

   people? _____

MANNERS
Made Easy

Lesson Three
HOW TO INTRODUCE OTHERS

Now that you know how to introduce yourself, you will learn how to introduce adults and friends to one another. The most important rule about introductions is to try. If you can't remember everyone's name, try anyway. Think of it as giving someone a present. When you give names to people who do not know one another, you make them feel more comfortable. Always begin the introduction using the most honored person's name first.

Here are the rules which clarify who is the most honored person.
1. Introduce the younger person to the older person (honored).
2. Introduce a male to a female (honored).
3. Introduce the less-distinguished person to the more distinguished person (honored).
4. Give first and last names if you can.

Turn first toward the person in the "honored" position. Address this person as
    "Grandmother, Reverend, Brother Smith, Mr. or Mrs. Jones."
    Example: Say "Grandmother, this is my friend from school, Laura Andrews."
(Always say the last name.) Turn to Laura and say, "Laura, this is my Grandmother, Mrs. Jenson." Because your grandmother's name may be different from yours, always use the last name when introducing people. Also, Laura would feel uncomfortable calling your grandmother, "Grandmother or Grandma."
    A good rule to remember when introducing people is to never use nicknames.

Example: Introducing your mother or father to your friend's parent (honored).

Give your parent's last name if it is different from yours. Start with the honored person and simply say, "I'd like to introduce _____ to you."

Example: Introducing your sibling to your friend (honored).

"Johnny, this is my sister, Amy." or "Amy, this is my brother, Johnny."

Example: Introducing your parent to your teacher (honored).

"Mrs. Hodges, I would like to introduce my mom, Jane Brown (or Mrs. Brown)." Your teacher may prefer to call your mom Mrs. or Ms. Brown, although they are both adults.

GREETINGS

You have been introduced to someone and now you must greet the new acquaintance.

Rule: USE FIVE OF THE SIX S's: Smile, Stand, See (eyes), Shake (hands), Say (your name)

• Say: "**Hello, Mr. or Mrs.____**" (The other S is "Say your name." In this situation, your name has already been given to the person you are meeting.)

• Your greeting after someone is introduced to you

"**Hello, it is nice to meet you, Mrs. Jenson.**" (Always say the person's name.)

If you have no help from the person who introduced you, ask a nice question, such as "Where do you go to school?" or make a statement about how you know the one who introduced you. Example: "John and I play on the same team."

• Your response as you walk away from someone you have just met

"**It was nice to meet you, Mrs. Jenson.**" (Use the person's name.)

• Always greet adults with a title such as Mr., Mrs., Miss, or Dr.

Sometimes when people are very close but are not relatives, parents permit their children to use an adult's first name. Other times adults have such long, difficult last names that students are permitted to use a title and the adult's first name such as Ms. Shannon (Waberloskivev).

• Greeting someone you already know

Simply say hello or hi along with their name and then make conversation.

Example: "Hello, Mary. How are things going with you?"

Hello, it is nice to meet you, Mrs. Jenson.

• **Greeting someone you already know but have not seen for a while.**

It is never polite or considerate to greet someone with "Hi, remember me?" Always give your name if you have not seen the person for a while. Think about how uncomfortable you would feel if you had to say, "No, I do not remember you."

   • **What happens if you are with a group of people you know, and a friend walks up who does not know the group?**

If the group is four or fewer people, you can name each person in the group to the friend, but if the group is large simply say your friend's name and let the others introduce themselves. Example: "This is my new neighbor, Hank McGrew." Someone in the group should use the six S's: "Hi Hank. I am Kerry Heath." Then the others should follow.

REMEMBERING NAMES

Do you ever have trouble remembering names? Everyone has trouble remembering them sometimes. What should you do if you forget someone's name and you need to introduce him or her to others?

Check one: _____ Make up a name and hope no one notices.

_____ Skip the introduction.

_____ Say, "I'm sorry, but I can't remember your name."

If you don't understand the name when you are introduced to someone, say "I didn't quite get your name" or "Could you repeat your name please?"

If someone mispronounces your name, politely correct them. Example: Your name is Jean but you are introduced as Jane. After the introduction, simply say, "It's Jean."

Write your own introduction of a close friend to your teacher.

_____

_____

_____

_____

ACTIVITY

Draw a crown over the word that describes the most honored person in each example, then write a proper introduction.

1. Introduce your classmate and your father. _____

_____

2. Introduce your mother and your classmate's mother. _____

_____

3. Introduce a male classmate and a female classmate. _____

_____

4. Introduce your father and your minister. _____

_____

CONVERSATION AFTER THE INTRODUCTION

Often it is difficult to know what to say or do after we have been introduced, said hello, and said the new acquaintance's name. The person making the introduction should tell you something about the other person, such as their relationship. Example: "This is my friend; my mom; my teacher." You may also tell how the introducer knows the individual or why the introducer wants you to meet the other person.

Write a phrase, sentence, or question that you might say to make conversation after you have said hello using the person's name. _____

_____

_____.

POINTS TO REMEMBER WHEN MAKING CONVERSATION

1. In a group, always try to include everyone in the conversation. Do not talk to only one person.
2. Listen and try not to interrupt.
3. Do not say something that might hurt someone's feelings.

MANNERS
Made Easy

LESSON THREE QUIZ

1. What is the most important rule about making introductions? _____

_____

2. What should you do if you cannot remember someone's name? _____

_____

3. Who wears the crown in any introduction? _____

4. What three factors determine who wears the crown? _____

_____

5. Why is it necessary to give the first and last name of a person? _____

_____

6. In a group, always try to include _____ in the conversation.

7. When talking with others, always listen and try not to _____ .

8. Do not say something that might _____ .

LESSON THREE BIBLE STUDY

KEY SCRIPTURE REFERENCE:

And he brought Simon to Jesus. When Jesus saw him, He said, "You are Simon, son of John. You will be called Cephas" (which means "Rock"). (John 1:42)

ADDITIONAL SCRIPTURE REFERENCE:

John 1:40-42

BIBLE LESSON:

John 1:40-42 is the story of two brothers, Andrew and Simon (Peter), who were fishermen. Andrew had heard Jesus speak and was so moved by Jesus' message, he wanted his brother Simon to meet Jesus. Andrew is mentioned only a few times in Scripture, but notice what an important thing he did. He brought his brother to meet the Lord Jesus. Jesus would later give Simon the name Peter, which means *rock*. Peter became one of Jesus' greatest followers. After Peter met Jesus, his goals and priorities changed. He was changed by Jesus' love and spent his life communicating that love to others.

Like Andrew, we must take seriously our responsibility to introduce people to each other. We never know how important that introduction might be.

BIBLE QUIZ

1. Why did Andrew want to introduce his brother to Jesus? _____

_____

2. Who would have been the most honored person when Andrew introduced his brother to Jesus?

_____

3. Write a possible introduction Andrew might have used. _____

_____

4. Did God have a plan for Peter's life? _____

Explain your answer. _____

_____

_____

Lesson Four
TELEPHONE MANNERS

Today we have cordless telephones, car phones, and cell phones. We all talk on the telephone and we all make an impression – a good one or a bad one. Our voice and choice of words are our only tools. When talking on the phone we either sound cold, unfriendly, and rude, or we sound warm, friendly, and alert.

Q&A

1. Can you name some adjectives to describe the impressions we often make while

    talking on the telephone?_____

2. Why are telephone manners so important? _____

3. Name some other types of telecommunication equipment we use today.

    _____

4. What rules do you have at your house about the use of the telephone?

    _____

5. To whom do you make phone calls? _____

6. Do you think you can hear a smile on the telephone? _____

    If not, try it with a classmate. You should hear a lift in your voice and a more pleasing tone when smiling.

ACTIVITY

Mark the parts of the following telephone conversation that are wrong.

____1. The telephone rings and your parent answers with "Hello."

____2. From a noisy background, your parent hears the caller say "Hey, is Danny around?"

____3. Your parent answers: "Danny can't come to the telephone right now."

____4. The caller says, "Don't you have a cordless phone you can take to him?"

____5. Your parent again says, "Danny can't talk on the phone now. Would you like to leave a message?"

____6. The caller says, "No!" Then your parent hears a loud click followed by a dial tone.

Now you will learn how to properly make a telephone call and how to avoid being rude on the phone.

HOW TO PROPERLY MAKE A TELEPHONE CALL

Here are the rules for the proper way to make a telephone call. The rules spell out TIME.

T ake the **Time** of day into consideration.

I dentify yourself and ask to speak to your friend.

M ake sure your friend can talk at this time.

E nd the conversation by saying good-bye first if you made the call.

Example: You are calling your friend Paul after school. (T) His mom answers the phone. If you recognize her voice, say, "Hello, Mrs. Randall. This is Joey. May I speak to Paul?" If you do not recognize the voice, say, "Hello, this is Joey. May I speak to Paul?" (I) When he comes to the phone, ask if this is a good time to talk. Say, "Can you talk now?" (M) End the conversation by saying good-bye first, because you made the call. (E)

Remember that someone else may need to use the phone at your house or your friend's house.

MANNERS
Made Easy

HOW TO PROPERLY ANSWER THE TELEPHONE
Here are the rules for answering the telephone. The rules are made up of four S's.

1. **Smile** as you pick up the telephone.
2. **Say** "Hello" (or whatever your parents teach you to say) in a polite tone of voice.
3. **Say,** "May I tell _____ who is calling?" if the caller does not identify himself or herself, but asks to speak to someone in your home.
4. **Say,** "_____is not available or is unable to come to the phone. May I take a message?" Write it down carefully. If you do not understand a word or the number, ask the caller to repeat it. Say, "Could you repeat that, please?"
   4a. Leave the message in a central location decided upon by your family. Messages can be very important.
   4b. If your parents are not at home, do not tell that to the caller. Instead say, "_____ is unable to come to the phone right now. May I take a message?" It is not necessary to lie when that person is not at home. Simply do not reveal that you are home alone.

Let's practice calling a friend.
Here are some sample dialogues.

Teacher rings a bell. Ring, ring.

First Student:	Hello.
Second Student: (Caller)	Hi. This is _____. May I please speak to _____? (the first student's name)
First Student:	This is _____. (the first student)
Second Student: (Caller)	I am calling to see if you know our assignment in our *Manners Made Easy* book.
First Student:	Yes, it is lesson four.
Second Student: (Caller)	Thanks. I'll see you at school tomorrow. Good-bye.
Kelly:	Hello.
Kari:	Hello, this is Kari. May I speak to Allison?
Kelly:	Yes, Kari, I will get her for you (or) I'm sorry Kari. She is not available.
Kari:	Thank you. I'll wait (or) I will call back. Good-bye.
Brian:	Hello.
Jimmy:	Hello, this is Jimmy. Is this Brian?
Brian:	Yes, Jimmy, how are you?
Jimmy:	I'm fine. Can you talk a few minutes?

Let's practice answering the phone when your parents are not home.

Teacher rings a bell. Ring, ring,

Student:	Hello.
Adult:	Hi. This is Sam Brown. Is your dad home?
Student:	I'm sorry. He can't come to the phone now.
	May I take a message?
Adult:	No, thank you. I will call back. Good-bye.

For more practice: Rewrite the following incorrect telephone conversations:

Kari:	Put Allison on the phone.
Kelly:	No. (Slams the phone down.)

_____

_____

_____

_____

Jimmy:	Hey Brian!
Brian:	What?
Jimmy:	How are you? This is Jimmy.
Brian:	Well, what do you want?

_____

_____

_____

_____

CALL-WAITING AND OTHER CONVENIENCES/ANNOYANCES

Call-Waiting Rules:

- When you are talking to a friend and you hear a beep, ask permission from the first caller to answer the other call. Do not say, "Hey, wait a minute" and then click over to the other call.
- Tell the second caller, if it is one of your friends, that you are on the other line and ask if you may please call him or her back. The priority is the first caller.
- If the second call turns out to be for one of your parents, ask the second caller to please hold while you get your parent. Go back to the first caller and tell him or her that a call has come in for your parent and you will have to call them back.
- Remember that you are the role model for others in your family.

Cellular Telephone Rules:

- Do not ask adults if you may use their cell phone unless it is an emergency. The owner usually pays for each call.
- If the adult offers to let you use the cell phone, keep your conversation as brief as possible.

Using the Telephone in Someone Else's Home

- Always ask permission before using the telephone.
- Keep your conversation brief.

Answering Machine Rules:

- Wait for the beep.
- Identify yourself.
- Give the time and day. (Sometimes the residents are out of town for a few days.)
- Say the person's name you are leaving the message for and then leave a short message, including your phone number.

Recording Your Outgoing Message

Do not record music such as your favorite song. Do not try to be cute or entertaining. Be brief. Example: "Hello, you have reached 000-555-2000. Please leave your message after the tone. Thank you."

Q&A
List some examples of inappropriate behavior while talking on the phone.

_____

_____

LESSON FOUR QUIZ

1. Name the things you need to work on most after studying this lesson. You may have one thing or as many as ten. _____

_____

2. What do the letters TIME stand for?

T _____

I _____

M _____

E _____

3. What things make the most difference in the impression we make on the phone?

_____

4. What should you say if you are home alone and someone calls for one of your parents?

_____

5. Why should you ask the person you are calling if this is a good time to talk?

_____

6. Who ends the conversation by saying good-bye first? _____

7. When a second caller beeps in on call-waiting, who should get your attention?

_____

8. What two things are important to remember about using someone else's phone?

_____ and _____

MANNERS
Made Easy

 ## LESSON FOUR BIBLE STUDY

KEY SCRIPTURE REFERENCE:

Let the words of my mouth, and the meditation of my heart, be acceptable in thy sight, O Lord, my strength, and my redeemer. (Psalms 19:14 KJV)

ADDITIONAL SCRIPTURE REFERENCES:

Psalms 19:14, Psalms 39:1, Matthew 12:36, Luke 6:31, and Colossians 4:6

BIBLE LESSON:

The Bible has many references which give us guidance regarding what we say to others and how we say it. We know that how we talk to others reveals a great deal about ourselves. Jesus said the two greatest commandments in the Bible were to love your neighbor as yourself, and to love God with all your heart. These commandments should be the basis for all of our conversations.

BIBLE QUIZ

1. Rewrite Psalms 19:14 in your own words. _____

_____

2. Matthew 12:36 speaks of "careless" words we may have spoken. What are some

    kinds of careless words? _____

3. *Your speech should always be gracious, seasoned with salt, so that you may know how you should answer*

    each person. (Colossians 4:6)

    What does it mean to season your speech with salt? Could this mean two

    different things? _____

    _____

4. Read Psalms 39:1. How can you apply these verses when talking on the phone?

    _____

5. Does the Golden Rule apply when talking on the phone? Why? _____

    _____

Lesson Five
WRITING THANK-YOU NOTES

Everyone likes to get personal mail, like thank-you notes and invitations. Have you ever received a handwritten note or letter in the mail? Perhaps a grandparent has sent you one. It's almost as much fun to send them as it is to get them. It's important to have the paper you need and know the proper way to write a note.

Name some of the kinds of letters or notes you have received. _____

_____

Occasions for Writing Notes:

1. To thank someone for any type of gift (even if you said thanks in person)
2. The bread and butter note (note to the host/hostess after an overnight stay)
3. The invitation response (answering an R.S.V.P.)
4. For any special treat or favor received
5. To tell someone they did a good job

Others _____

Here is an example of a properly written thank-you note for a birthday present.

Dear Caleb,

    It was such fun having you at my birthday party. I really like the video you gave me. Our family has already enjoyed it several times. Every time I watch it, I will think of you. Maybe you can visit me soon and we will watch it together.

    Thank you for remembering me in such a special way.

                Your friend,
                Kevin Rawls

February 23, 2003

MANNERS
Made Easy

Notice the proper format for writing any kind of note, whether it is on a flat card or a piece of fold-over notepaper. There is always a salutation, the body or text of the note, the closing, your signature, and the date. For letters, write the date at the top.

(Salutation)
Dear_____, *(comma at the end)*
(Leave one line blank)
    (Indent for the body of the note)
....
....
....
    (Leave one line blank between the text and the closing)
    Yours truly, *(Capitalize only the first word of the closing)*

    Your Signature
(Leave one line blank)
February 23, 2003 *(Date)*

Here is an example of a properly addressed envelope.

Kevin Rawls	Postage Stamp
85 Melba Drive	*(first class)*
Maintown, AZ 00000	
Mr. Caleb Barnes	
43 Cherry Place	
Maintown, AZ 00000	

Here are some important guidelines for writing thank-you notes.

1. If possible, buy notepaper or cards without Thank You preprinted on them. If you must use notes with Thank You on preprinted on them, do not begin writing your thank-you note with thank you. Notice the note to Caleb starts with the word *It*, which is always proper. An example is: It was nice of you to…

2. In your own words, tell how much you appreciate their thoughtfulness.

3. If you don't like the gift, do not say so. You can always find something good to say about it, such as, "Thank you for your thoughtfulness in choosing _____ for me."

4. Always name the gift and tell how you plan to use it. If the gift is money, it is better not to mention the amount. If the note is for a kind act or favor, mention it.

5. Write the note as soon as possible, but remember it is never too late to write one. You may apologize for sending it late, but do not make excuses.

6. Short, handwritten notes are preferred over preprinted, typed, or e-mailed ones.

Answering an invitation that has R.S.V.P. printed at the bottom

The term R.S.V.P. on invitations that we receive is French for *Répondez s'il vous plaît!* In English it means *Answer, please.* You must answer such an invitation with yes or no unless the R.S.V.P. says "regrets only." Then it is not necessary to respond unless you cannot attend. The host will assume you are coming. If there is a telephone number after R.S.V.P., you may call to give your answer. Written replies to invitations may be written on the same kind of paper you use to write other notes and in much the same format.

Example:

I am sorry that I will be unable to come to your party. It sounds like great fun.
I hope you have a wonderful celebration.

You may give the reason why you cannot come with a simple explanation such as, "I will be out of town," but giving that information is not required.

In a situation where the host does not include a reply card and envelope, you will need to send one. For this type of correspondence, you may have your name printed on the front of your notes or cards, or you may simply buy plain or decorated ones. Discount and grocery stores usually sell plain, inexpensive packages or boxes of notes and envelopes.

MANNERS
Made Easy

LESSON FIVE QUIZ

1. Name some of the times you should write notes. _____

_____

2. For a thank-you note, what kind of card or notepaper should you look for?

_____

3. What does the French term R.S.V.P. mean in English? _____

4. Why do you think it is important not to tell someone you do not like their gift?

_____

5. What should you always mention in a thank-you note? _____

_____

# Lesson Five Bible Study

KEY SCRIPTURE REFERENCE:

I write these things to you, hoping to come to you soon. But if I should be delayed, I have written so that you will know how people ought to act in God's household, which is the church of the living God, the pillar and foundation of the truth. (I Timothy 3:14-15)

ADDITIONAL SCRIPTURE REFERENCES:

Acts 15:23, Romans 15:15, I Cor. 4:14, II Cor. 3:1-3, Gal. 6:11, Phil. 3:1

BIBLE LESSON:

Today we know much about the Apostles because of the many letters they wrote. Paul wrote more than 10 of the New Testament books as letters of encouragement and instruction to churches. Others were written by John, James, Peter, and Jude. These letters are called epistles, which is a written message sent as a means of communication between persons separated by distance. Most of Paul's letters followed the same format we still use today; a salutation, body, and closing.

Even in biblical times the function of the salutation or greeting was to establish a relationship between the sender and the addressee. The body of the letter was to communicate the message, and the closing again highlighted the relationship between the sender and addressee.

In his second letter to the church at Corinth, Paul said that we are the living letters of the message of Christ.

In this lesson we have learned how important our written notes and letters can be to others.

BIBLE QUIZ

1. Many of the New Testament books are letters to churches. Who wrote most of these letters?

_____ What are the names of three of Paul's epistles or letters?

_____

2. What are the three parts of a letter? _____

3. Summarize the salutation and closing of one of Paul's letters. _____

_____

4. Why is it so important to properly write notes and letters? _____

_____

Lesson Six
TABLE MANNERS

Did you ever eat dinner with a two-year old? If you have, you have seen food smeared over their face, food on the floor, knocked-over milk glasses, and all kinds of messes. It's not a pretty sight, but we don't expect more from two-year olds, because they haven't yet learned good table manners.

Have you ever been embarrassed because you did not know the right way to eat something? Embarrassment can be painful, especially when it happens to us. When you go to dinner with people outside your family, you will want to know all that you will learn in this lesson. The way you conduct yourself around food has a big influence on how you will be accepted as a date and for getting a job when you are old enough. Learning table manners can be fun, and you will use them all your life. The first thing we will learn is how to set the table properly.

SETTING THE TABLE

The way the forks, knives, spoons, glasses, cups, plates, bowls, and napkins are arranged on the tablecloth or placemat is called a "place setting." The illustration below is a simple place setting. Label the pieces included in a simple place setting.

LEARNING THE NAPKIN RULES

1. Place the napkin in your lap with the folded edge toward the knees. When you lift the napkin by the folded edge and use it to wipe your mouth, you will not get any food stains on your clothes when you replace it in your lap.
2. Use it to dab your mouth.
3. Dab your mouth with it before drinking from a glass so smudges will not be on the glass.
4. Leave the napkin in your lap until you get up to leave the table. When you are temporarily away from the table and when you leave for the last time, place the used napkin to the left of your plate or in your chair. Never refold a napkin.
5. Never put a napkin on a plate.

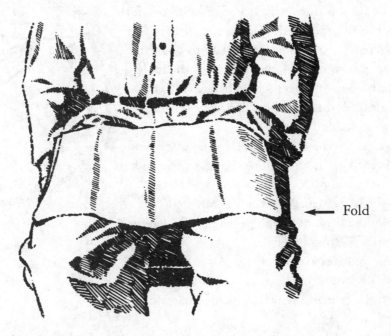

← Fold

GOING THROUGH A MEAL

1. A gentleman seats the lady on his right, and then any others who do not have a male escort.
2. Watch the hostess before touching anything. Do things in the same order the hostess does them.
3. The host or hostess may choose to say grace before the meal.
4. Hostess puts her napkin in her lap with the folded edge toward her knees.
5. Host or hostess will begin passing food and condiments to the right.
6. Prepare your beverage. If you use lemon in your drink, use your left hand to cover the right hand while you squeeze the lemon wedge.
7. Place the sugar or sweetener packet on the bread and butter plate or neatly on the table. Don't crumple it or put it under the rim of your plate.

8. Place the iced teaspoon on the opened sweetener packet or turn the spoon bowl-side down and prop it on the rim of a plate. The iced teaspoon is the only utensil you can prop. This avoids getting tea stains on the tablecloth.

9. Butter one half or one bite of the bread at a time, never the entire roll or slice. Then place the used knife across the top of the plate with the cutting edge toward you.

10. Cut one or two bites of meat at a time. Place the dinner knife as described above.

11. If the salad is served before the main course, there will be a salad fork to the left of the dinner fork.

12. If the salad is served with the meal, use the dinner fork.

13. When resting or drinking, the silverware should be placed as shown in illustration A.

14. When the meal is finished, place your knife and fork as shown in illustration B. Make sure they are far enough from the top edge of the plate to be secure when the hostess removes the plate from the table.

15. Use your napkin often, especially before drinking from a glass. Return it to your lap with the fold toward your knees.

16. Keep your napkin in your lap unless you must excuse yourself temporarily, or until the hostess removes hers from her lap and places it to the left of the place setting signaling that the meal is completed.

17. Never refold a napkin. Simply place it unfolded to the left of your place setting.

18. Never put your napkin on a plate. An exception to this is at a formal dinner, when the napkin may be placed in the center of the clean plate as part of the place setting.

19. Never put used silverware back on the table.

20. If you drop a knife, fork, or spoon, politely ask the hostess for another one. You may pick up a dropped napkin.

A.

B.

LEARNING CORRECT DINING MANNERS

1. Label each piece of the full place setting according to the illustration

2. Label each piece of the simple place setting according to the illustration.

3. A dinner napkin is opened halfway and placed in the lap with the fold toward the knees, as shown in the illustration. When the diner picks it up, uses it, and replaces it, the napkin will not leave food stains or smudges on the lap of the diner.

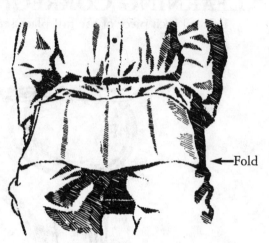

←Fold

4. Each utensil should be picked up and held like a pencil, as shown in the illustration. Continental-style eating is done with the inverted fork in the left hand. The knife remains in the right hand. Both American and Continental ways of eating are correct in our country. Eating Continental-style also permits the diner to place the forearms on the table. In the American style of eating we place the left arm in the lap at all times unless we need to cut the entrée, butter bread, pass something, or use the napkin.

5. Practice the correct way to cut your food. Refer to the two illustrations at the bottom of the page. Two additional cutting mistakes to watch for are the "cello method" which draws the elbows up toward one's neighbor, and the "tip of the fork" or "dainty" method in which the diner tries to hold the fork by the tip of the handle with just the thumb and two fingertips.

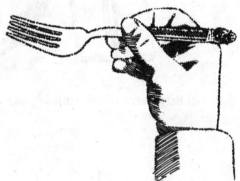

Correct   Incorrect

6. The term *gangplanking* refers to resting the tip of the handle of a utensil on the table with the point of the bowl or tines of the utensil resting on the plate. Only the iced teaspoon may be propped in that fashion to keep tea stains off the tablecloth. It is never proper to gangplank any of the other utensils.

Incorrect   Correct

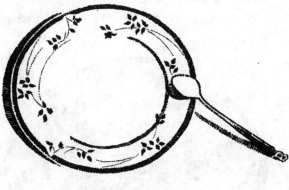

7. When finished eating, place the knife above the fork in a 10:00 to 4:00 position as shown in the illustration. The utensils should be placed securely on the plate so they won't fall off when the plate is removed by the hostess.

8. Waving and talking with your silverware is dangerous and unpleasant for others to see.

9. Keep your elbows close to your sides even while cutting up food.

10. Dip soup away from yourself, gently scraping the bowl of the spoon across the back of the soup bowl to catch any drips.

11. The spoon should never be left in the soup bowl during the course or when you finish. Leaving a handle protruding upward from a bowl is dangerous. You might bump the handle and flip the spoon out of the bowl.

12. Place a soup spoon on the service plate beneath the bowl, as shown in illustration A.

13. Never leave a spoon protruding from a glass. You might poke yourself in the eye. Place the tip of the spoon on the rim of a plate. The back of the spoon should be turned upward.

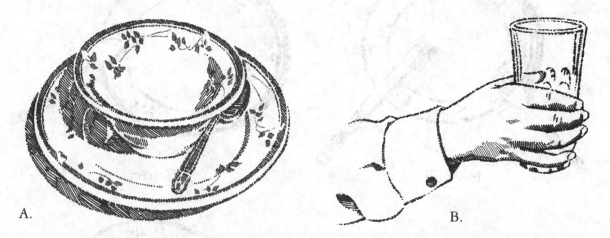

A.   B.

14. Never touch the rim of a glass or cup with your hands, as shown in illustration B.

15. Slurping drinks is annoying to others.

16. Shoveling food and bending down to meet the plate is impolite and unappetizing to others.

17. Don't scrape your plate clean.

18. Elbows should not be on a table when food is present.

19. Taking food out of your mouth with your hand is unpleasant to all. Cover your mouth with your hand or napkin and remove the food with the utensil you used to put it in your mouth. Then place the unwanted item on your plate, preferably under something like the garnish. If you place it under the rim of your plate and the plate is subsequently removed, you expose the ugly mess.

20. Talking with food in your mouth is most unpleasant for others to see.

21. If you are offered something you cannot eat, simply say "No thank you" or "Thank you, I don't care for any."

22 Taking the last piece of food from a plate or platter is rude.

23. Taking too much food at a time is rude. You should consider how many other people will need to take a serving.

24. Passing food to the right around a table the first
    time permits diners to take a dish with the
    left hand, serve themselves with their
    right hand, and pass it on, as shown
    in illustration A. After food makes
    one trip around the table, you may
    pass it the shortest way to a fellow
    diner who asks for another serving.

25. Never use your own utensil to take
    food from a common dish on the table.
    If there is not a serving fork or spoon, you
    may ask the hostess for one.

26. Reaching across the table to get something is rude.
    You might knock something over. Politely ask
    someone to pass something to you.

A.

27. Licking a bowl, plate, or utensil is
    unhealthy and unappetizing to others.

28. The salt and pepper should always be
    passed together, as shown in
    illustration B, even if only one was
    requested.

29. Picking one's teeth with a toothpick in
    public is very unappealing to others.

30. If you have something stuck in your teeth,
    excuse yourself and take care of the problem
    in private.

31. Don't say "yuck" at the table.

B.

32. Burping with your mouth open is very rude and unpleasant to others.

33. When a gentleman is seating a lady, she should back up to the chair so that the back of
    her knees touch the front of the chair. Then she lowers herself straight into the chair.
    She places her hands on the sides of the chair and helps the gentleman move the chair
    forward under the table.

MANNERS
Made Easy

LESSON SIX QUIZ

1. What are some of the nice things men and boys can do for ladies? _____

   doors and _____ ladies with their chairs. The girls should say "_____."

2. Name some things you should not talk about at the table.

   _____.

3. Do not _____ your teeth at the table or in public.

4. Why do we have table manners? To make everyone's meal _____.

5. Cut _____ or two bites of meat at a time. Why?

   So your food won't look _____ and won't get _____.

6. Is it all right to tilt your chair back? _____ Why? _____

7. You should never put your napkin on your _____.

8. What should you do about dental appliances such as retainers? They should be _____

   out before you sit down to eat, and put in a pocket or purse.

9. Never talk with _____in your mouth. Never _____ with your silverware.

10. What do you say if you don't like something served to you? "I don't _____ for any."

11. Why should you dip soup away from you? So you don't _____ it.

12. _____ off one bite at a time from a roll or large piece of bread.

13. Never take the _____ piece of _____ from a dish or platter.

14. Pass any food or _____ to the person on your right.

15. Never _____ down until everyone is at the table. Seat the _____ first.

16. Never leave a _____ sticking up from a glass or bowl.

17. Start eating with the silverware from the _____ and use the utensils moving inward

   toward the plate.

18. Boys and men should always _____ their _____ or _____

   before entering a building or sitting down to eat. Exception: when you are in a gymnasium.

19. You should always push your _____ back under the table when you get up for any reason.

20. When you finish eating, you should wait until everyone finishes before _____

   the table.

21. Which way should the cutting edge of the knife be turned when you place it on your plate?

   Toward the _____.

22. When you finish eating, place your knife and fork in a _____ position.

   Place the _____ above the fork.

23. You should say "yes" or "no" or "yes ma'am" or "no ma'am." What are some things you should

   not say? _____

   _____

24. When you go to a party or to visit, you should always say "_____" to

   the parent or the chaperone as soon as you arrive, and say "_____ for

   inviting me" when you leave.

25. When you are an overnight guest, you should pick up your _____ and

   _____ the bed.

26. What should you do if someone says something funny about you? _____ or

_____ them.

27. What are some things you should never do to other people? _____

_____

28. Is etiquette just a lot of rules to learn or is there a reason for the rules?

_____

29. What are some reasons for rules of etiquette? _____

_____

LESSON SIX BIBLE STUDY

KEY SCRIPTURE REFERENCE:

But when you are invited, go and recline in the lowest place, so that when the one who invited you comes, he will say to you, 'Friend, move up higher.' You will then be honored in the presence of all the other guests. (Luke 14:10)

ADDITIONAL SCRIPTURE REFERENCES:

I Kings 17:7-15, Matt. 6:11, Luke 14: 8-14, Luke 22:14-20, and John 21:1-14

BIBLE LESSON:

In the Old Testament, the prophet Elijah asked a widow to prepare a meal for him. When she responded that she had only a cup of flour and bit of oil left, Elijah told her that her obedience would result in an unending supply of flour and oil. She obeyed and never ran out of food again.

In Luke 14, Jesus uses the parable of a great banquet to teach His followers to show kindness and consideration to others. Jesus says that as a guest you should consider that other guests may be more important than you are. In Luke 14:11 He says, *"For everyone who exalts himself will be humbled, and the one who humbles himself will be exalted."*

BIBLE QUIZ

1. Read the story of Elijah and the widow from I Kings 17:7-15. What lesson can we learn about

   sharing a meal with others? _____

2. Write in your own words what Jesus was trying to teach His followers in the parable of the great

   banquet. _____

3. Read John 21:1-14 which tells about the meal Jesus prepared for His disciples. How long had

   the disciples been fishing? _____

4. What did Jesus tell them to do when they said they hadn't caught any fish?

   _____

5. Knowing that Jesus was their Savior and Lord, how do you think the disciples felt about Jesus

   cooking breakfast for them? _____

   _____

MOUTH MANNERS AND OTHER COURTESIES

Here are rules for general good manners and common courtesies in a social setting.

1. Never put your feet on the furniture. Keep them on the floor.
2. Never pick at your toes or fingernails in public.
3. Excessive scratching of your head in public is unsanitary.
4. Combing or brushing your hair in public is unsanitary. Excuse yourself to take care of it in private.
5. Picking at your ears is very unpleasant to others.
6. Coughing without covering your mouth is unsanitary and spreads germs. Always cover your mouth, preferably with a tissue.
7. Yawning with your mouth open and uncovered is unpleasant for others.
8. Picking your nose is disgusting to others. It is also unsanitary.
9. Sneezing without covering your mouth is unhealthy. If you are at a dining table, you may use your napkin if you do not have time to reach for a tissue or a handkerchief.
10. Wiping your nose on your arm or sleeve is not sanitary. Excuse yourself, go to the restroom, and blow your nose.
11. Opening a door for someone is kind and helpful.
12. Saying, "I'm sorry" shows concern for others.
13. Laughing at others hurts their feelings.
14. Talking in church or in the movies disturbs others.
15. Gossiping is unkind and hurtful. The gossip is often untrue, but even if you know the topic to be true, it is still wrong to gossip. Think about the Golden Rule.
16. Interrupting is rude. Wait until the person is finished talking on the telephone. If you have an urgent message, you may look them in the eye to get their attention. Then say "Excuse me" before relaying the message.
17. Always push your chair back under a table or desk.
18. Never point or stare at people. Don't walk in front of people. Don't whisper in front of people.
19. Say "Excuse me" anytime you must leave the company of others.

HOW TO PROPERLY ANSWER THE TELEPHONE

Here are the rules for answering the telephone. The rules are made up of four S's.

1. **Smile** as you pick up the telephone.

2. **Say** "Hello" (or whatever your parents teach you to say) in a polite tone of voice.

3. **Say**, "May I tell _____ who is calling?" if the caller does not identify himself or herself, but asks to speak to someone in your home.

4. **Say**, "_____ is not available or is unable to come to the phone. May I take a message?" Write it down carefully. If you do not understand a word or the number, ask the caller to repeat it. Say, "Could you repeat that, please?"

4a. Leave the message in a central location decided upon by your family. Messages can be very important.

4b. If your parents are not at home, do not tell that to the caller. Instead say, "_____ is unable to come to the phone right now. May I take a message?" It is not necessary to lie when that person is not at home. Simply do not reveal that you are home alone.

ACTIVITY

Ask for two volunteers. Tell them to bring their student sheet with them so they can follow the dialogue. Using the two pieces of cardboard, place the 'Caller' sign by one phone and the 'Receiver' sign by the other. Practice the role-playing dialogues using each student in the classroom.

First Student:	Hello.
Second Student: (Caller)	Hi. This is _____. May I please speak to _____? (the first student's name)
First Student:	This is _____. (the first student)
Second Student: (Caller)	I am calling to see if you know our assignment in our Manners Made Easy book.
First Student:	Yes, it is lesson four.
Second Student: (Caller)	Thanks. I'll see you at school tomorrow. Good-bye.

Kelly:	Hello.
Kari:	Hello, this is Kari. May I speak to Allison?
Kelly:	Yes, Kari, I will get her for you (or) I'm sorry Kari. She is not available.
Kari:	Thank you. I'll wait (or) I will call back. Good-bye.

Brian:	Hello.
Jimmy:	Hello, this is Jimmy. Is this Brian?
Brian:	Yes, Jimmy, how are you?
Jimmy:	I'm fine. Can you talk a few minutes?

Have students rewrite the rude phone conversations which appear on student page 19.

CALL-WAITING AND OTHER CONVENIENCES/ANNOYANCES

Review these four rules about call-waiting.
- When you are talking to a friend and you hear a beep, ask permission from the first caller to answer the other call. Do not say, "Hey, wait a minute" and then click over to the other call.
- Tell the second caller, if it is one of your friends, that you are on the other line and ask if you may please call him or her back. The priority is the first caller.
- If the second call turns out to be for one of your parents, ask the second caller to please hold while you get your parent. Go back to the first caller and tell him or her that a call has come for your parent and you will have to call them back.
- Remember that you are the role model for others in your family.

Cellular Telephone Rules

- Do not ask adults if you may use their cell phone unless it is an emergency. The owner usually pays for each call.
- If the adult offers to let you use the cell phone, keep your conversation as brief as possible.

Using the Telephone in Someone Else's Home
- Always ask permission before using the telephone.
- Keep your conversation brief.

Answering Machine Rules
- Wait for the beep.
- Identify yourself.
- Give the time and day. (Sometimes the residents are out of town for a few days.)
- Say the person's name you are leaving the message for and then leave a short message, including your phone number.

Recording Your Outgoing Message
Do not record music such as your favorite song. Do not try to be cute or entertaining. Be brief. Example: "Hello, you have reached 000-555-2000. Please leave your message after the tone. Thank you."

Behavior Inappropriate When Talking on the Telephone
Ask students to give examples of inappropriate behavior, then add these to them: lying, interrupting, not talking clearly into the mouthpiece, hanging up too quickly, eating, drinking, chewing gum, making noise, talking to someone in the room, gossiping, staying on the phone too long, leaving the television or radio on too loud, etc.

LESSON FOUR QUIZ

1. Name the things you need to work on most after studying this lesson. You may have one thing or as many as ten. **(Varies)**

2. What do the letters TIME stand for? **(Take the time of day into consideration. Identify yourself. Make sure your friend can talk. End the conversation if you made the call.)**

3. What things make the most difference in the impression we make on the phone? **(Smile, tone of voice, choice of words, attitude, interest, etc.)**

4. What should you say if you are home alone and someone calls for one of your parents? **(I'm sorry. He/she cannot come to the phone right now. May I take a message?)**

5. Why should you ask the person you are calling if this is a good time to talk? **(The person you are calling may be busy.)**

6. Who ends the conversation by saying good-bye first? **(The caller)**

7. When a second caller beeps in on call-waiting, who should get your attention? **(The first caller, unless you are simply chatting with a friend and an important call comes in.)**

8. What two things are important to remember about using someone else's phone? **(Ask permission and keep your conversation brief.)**

 ## LESSON FOUR BIBLE STUDY

KEY SCRIPTURE REFERENCE:

Let the words of my mouth, and the meditation of my heart, be acceptable in thy sight, O Lord, my strength, and my redeemer. (Psalms 19:14 KJV)

ADDITIONAL SCRIPTURE REFERENCES:

Psalms 19:14, Psalms 39:1, Matthew 12:36, Luke 6:31, and Colossians 4:6

BIBLE LESSON:

The Bible has many references which give us guidance regarding what we say to others and how we say it. We know that how we talk to others reveals a great deal about ourselves. Jesus said the two greatest commandments in the Bible were to love your neighbor as yourself, and to love God with all your heart. These commandments should be the basis for all of our conversations.

BIBLE QUIZ

1. Rewrite Psalms 19:14 in your own words.
2. Matthew 12:36 speaks of "careless" words we may have spoken. What are some kinds of careless words? (**Making fun of others, gossiping about others, lying, swearing, etc.**)
3. *Your speech should always be gracious, seasoned with salt, so that you may know how you should answer each person.* (Colossians 4:6)
   What does it mean to season your speech with salt? Could this mean two different things? (**First, salt preserves food and keeps it from spoiling. Second, salt adds flavor to many foods, making them taste better. Our words need to be pleasant and not leave a bad taste.**)
4. Read Psalms 39:1. How can you apply these verses when talking on the phone?
5. Does the Golden Rule apply when talking on the phone? Why? (**Yes, because we want to be treated with respect.**)

Lesson Five
WRITING THANK-YOU NOTES

LESSON OVERVIEW
This lesson has five main topics:
- Introduction about writing notes
- Occasions for writing notes
- A properly written thank-you note for a birthday present
- Examples of how to write notes and address envelopes
- Guidelines, R.S.V.P., and tips

SUPPLIES NEEDED
- Fold-over note and envelope or a flat card with an envelope for each student
- For practice they may cut a sheet of notebook paper in half and then fold it once to look similar to a fold-over note. It should stand on its open edges like a tent.

ABOUT THIS LESSON

Writing thank-you notes of any kind has almost become a lost art. However, with a renewed emphasis on the need for good manners, the practice is returning. By teaching students how to write thank-you notes and how to choose the right kind of paper to use, you are helping them develop a habit that will reinforce the Golden Rule. When the students hear someone say, "Oh, I got your note. Thanks!" they will feel good about themselves. Although it may appear to be a selfish motive, writing notes will help students portray a positive image in both social and business worlds. Writing thank-you notes can make a difference in whether someone is invited back socially. In business, writing notes and using other good manners can influence an employer to hire someone or give him or her a raise.

TEACHING THE LESSON

Prior to the class, you will need to get or to make two sample thank-you notes, with matching envelopes. One should be flat and one folded, as described in the supplies box.

Begin the lesson by letting the students tell about a letter or note they have received in the mail and how it made them feel. Let students discuss thank-you notes they have written. Tell the students that after reviewing the student worksheets, they will actually be writing notes of their own. Hold up the note written to Caleb (student page 23) and explain that it is written on the inside of the folded note. If the outside top of the note is void of any indentation or decoration, writers may begin at the top of the inside of the unfolded notepaper. If there is any indentation or decoration on the front, leave the inside top of the notepaper blank and begin writing below the inside crease. Finishing the note on the back side is permitted but not preferred. Once the note is written, insert it into the envelope so that when the receiver removes the note from the envelope, flap side up, the note is ready to open and read.

When a flat card is used, write the note on the front side of the card. The handwritten side of the card goes into the envelope facing the person inserting it. When the receiver opens the envelope, the written side comes out facing him or her and is ready to read.

Children are never too young to learn to send thank-you notes. The following example is an appropriate thank-you note for very young students.

Note: For students who cannot write well, the parent can write a few words and have the child sign it or draw a picture.

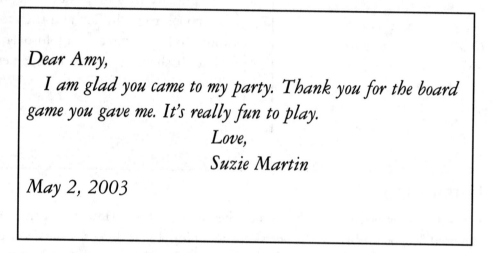

Dear Amy,
I am glad you came to my party. Thank you for the board game you gave me. It's really fun to play.
Love,
Suzie Martin

May 2, 2003

Here are some important guidelines for writing thank-you notes.

1. If possible, buy notepaper or cards without Thank You preprinted on them. If you must use notes with Thank You preprinted on them, do not begin writing your thank-you note with thank you. Notice the note on student page 23 starts with the word *It*, which is always proper. An example is: It was nice of you to…

2. In your own words, tell how much you appreciate their thoughtfulness.

3. If you don't like the gift, do not say so. You can always find something good to say about it, such as, "Thank you for your thoughtfulness in choosing____for me."

4. Always name the gift and tell how you plan to use it. If the gift is money, it is better not to mention the amount. If the note is for a kind act or favor, mention it.

5. Write the note as soon as possible, but remember it is never too late to write one. You may apologize for sending it late, but do not make excuses.

6. Short, handwritten notes are preferred over preprinted, typed, or e-mailed ones.

PRACTICE

Before the students write on their new thank-you note, have them practice on notebook paper. Check their format and spelling. Let them copy the note onto their notepaper or card. For this learning experience, they may wish to use a pencil to correct any mishaps and still have a neat and clean note.

Direct students through an exercise with everyone writing the same note on notebook paper. Notebook paper can be used to practice addressing the envelope. Then have each student write a note to another person in the class thanking him or her for something nice he or she has done. Example: lending pencils, being a friend, helping with a project.

Have each student write notes and address the envelopes to their parents. They can take them home with them. Other people to write may include: a schoolteacher, the principal, a teacher at church, or a relative. It should not be difficult to find something to thank anyone for. People always enjoy being thanked for their time and efforts on someone's behalf.

R.S.V.P is French for *Répondez, s'il vous plaît* and means *Answer, please.* The French are so polite they always add please to a request. For advanced students, you may ask them to answer an invitation with R.S.V.P. on it.

E-mail rules:

Internet and e-mail messages are not included in the student pages, but students are using the internet to communicate with their friends. There are a few rules they should observe.

1. Capitalization and spelling count the same as in handwritten correspondence. Writing in all capitalized letters is rude. It makes the reader feel the writer is shouting at them.

2. Only words that are proper to say face-to-face or in public should be sent. Remember that other eyes may see the message on the screen.

3. Brief, to-the-point messages are always better.

4. It's better to ask "May we exchange e-mail addresses?" than to ask "What's your e-mail address?"

5. Always ask about a friend's house rules regarding receiving e-mail messages. For example, don't send long attachments that take up hard drive space unless the recipient says you may.

6. Do not give out a friend's e-mail address without their permission.

MANNERS
Made Easy

LESSON FIVE QUIZ

1. Name some of the times you should write notes. (**When you've received a gift, when someone has hosted a party, when someone does something nice for you, etc.**)
2. For a thank-you note, what kind of card or notepaper should you look for? (**One without Thank You preprinted on the front**)
3. What does the French term R.S.V.P. mean in English? (**Answer, please**)
4. Why do you think it is important not to tell someone you do not like their gift? (**It would hurt their feelings**)
5. What should you always mention in a thank-you note? (**The gift or the act of kindness**)

 # Lesson Five Bible Study

KEY SCRIPTURE REFERENCE:

I write these things to you, hoping to come to you soon. But if I should be delayed, I have written so that you will know how people ought to act in God's household, which is the church of the living God, the pillar and foundation of the truth. (I Timothy 3:14-15)

ADDITIONAL SCRIPTURE REFERENCES:

Acts 15:23, Romans 15:15, I Cor. 4:14, II Cor. 3:1-3, Gal. 6:11, Phil. 3:1

BIBLE LESSON:

Today we know much about the Apostles because of the many letters they wrote. Paul wrote more than 10 of the New Testament books as letters of encouragement and instruction to churches. Others were written by John, James, Peter, and Jude. These letters are called epistles, which is a written message sent as a means of communication between persons separated by distance. Most of Paul's letters followed the same format we still use today; a salutation, body, and closing.

Even in biblical times the function of the salutation or greeting was to establish a relationship between the sender and the addressee. The body of the letter was to communicate the message, and the closing again highlighted the relationship between the sender and addressee.

In his second letter to the church at Corinth, Paul said that we are the living letters of the message of Christ.

In this lesson we have learned how important our written notes and letters can be to others.

BIBLE QUIZ

1. Many of the New Testament books are letters to churches. Who wrote most of these letters? (**Paul**) What are the names of three of Paul's epistles or letters? (**Romans, Corinthians, Timothy**)
2. What are the three parts of a letter? (**Salutation, body, closing**)
3. Summarize the salutation and closing of one of Paul's letters.
4. Why is it so important to properly write notes and letters? (**Because they reflect who we are and communicate a personal message from us.**)

Lesson Six
TABLE MANNERS

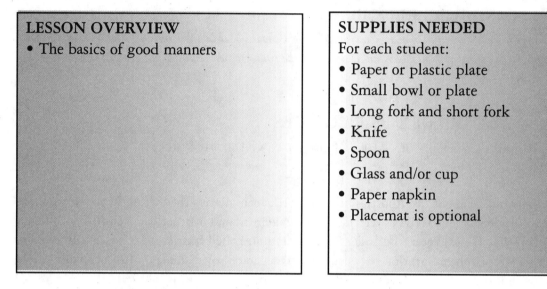

LESSON OVERVIEW
• The basics of good manners

SUPPLIES NEEDED
For each student:
• Paper or plastic plate
• Small bowl or plate
• Long fork and short fork
• Knife
• Spoon
• Glass and/or cup
• Paper napkin
• Placemat is optional

ABOUT THIS LESSON

Learning good table manners – no matter the age – must be a hands-on experience. With demonstrations, text, pictures, student participation, and practice, this lesson will be one of the most enjoyable. Begin by brainstorming what the students think about table manners and experiences they have had at the table. Go over the information on their first student page. Review the need for learning proper table manners.

TEACHING THE LESSON

SETTING THE TABLE

The way the forks, knives, spoons, glasses, cups, plates, bowls, and napkins are arranged on the tablecloth or placemat is called a "place setting." See the illustration below.

Begin by discussing the simplest place setting as shown on the previous page. The setting should have one dinner plate in the center near the edge of the table next to the student; one small salad bowl or plate to the left of the fork; one beverage glass at the top right of the plate; one knife next to the right side of the plate with the cutting edge toward the plate; one spoon to the right of the knife; one short-handled fork at the top of the plate (for dessert); and one long-handled fork to the left of the plate. The napkin is placed to the left of the fork or under the fork if space is limited. This setting is for salad served with the meal (hence no salad fork needed), entrée, beverage, and dessert. A place-mat (may be paper) may be used instead of a tablecloth.

For young students, a dinner plate, knife, fork, spoon, glass, and napkin may be enough. Ask the students to arrange their place setting according to the picture or demonstration.

Demonstrate how to hold the knife, fork, spoon, and glass. Refer to pictures in student pages. Ask the students to try it. Make sure the students are holding each utensil correctly. Bad habits are difficult to overcome.

DEMONSTRATE THE NAPKIN RULES.

1. Place the napkin in your lap with the folded edge toward the knees. When you lift the napkin by the folded edge and use it to wipe your mouth, you will not get any food stains on your clothes when you replace it in your lap.
2. Use it to dab your mouth.
3. Dab your mouth with it before drinking from a glass so smudges will not be on the glass.
4. Leave the napkin in your lap until you get up to leave the table. When you are temporarily away from the table and when you leave for the last time, place the used napkin to the left of your plate or in your chair. Never refold a napkin.
5. Never put a napkin on a plate.

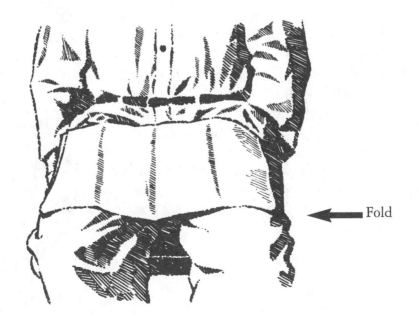
Fold

MANNERS
Made Easy

REVIEW

Bad habits can be broken only when they are reinforced with good ones. To teach table manners, use the illustrations from the student pages. Demonstrate each one yourself or assign a student to demonstrate them in front of the class. As you show the rude behavior, teach the remedy for it, asking students for suggestions.

GOING THROUGH A MEAL

This section may be taught with or without food. Arrange students around a table and go through the steps with the teacher playing the role of the hostess.

1. A gentleman seats the lady on his right, and then any others who do not have a male escort.
2. Watch the hostess before touching anything. Do things in the same order the hostess does them.
3. The host or hostess may choose to say grace before the meal.
4. Hostess puts her napkin in her lap with the folded edge toward her knees.
5. Host or hostess will begin passing food and condiments to the right.
6. Prepare your beverage. If you use lemon in your drink, use your left hand to cover the right hand while you squeeze the lemon wedge.
7. Place the sugar or sweetener packet on the bread and butter plate or neatly on the table. Don't crumple it or put it under the rim of your plate.
8. Place the iced teaspoon on the opened sweetener packet or turn the spoon bowl-side down and prop it on the rim of a plate. The iced teaspoon is the only utensil you can prop. This avoids getting tea stains on the tablecloth.
9. Butter one half or one bite of the bread at a time, never the entire roll or slice. Then place the used knife across the top of the plate with the cutting edge toward you.
10. Cut one or two bites of meat at a time. Place the dinner knife as described above.
11. If the salad is served before the main course, there will be a salad fork to the left of the dinner fork.
12. If the salad is served with the meal, use the dinner fork.
13. When resting or drinking, the silverware should be placed as shown in illustration A.
14. When the meal is finished, place your knife and fork as shown in illustration B. Make sure they are far enough from the top edge of the plate to be secure when the hostess removes the plate from the table.

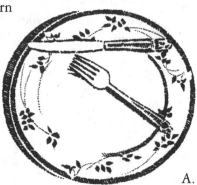

A.

B.

15. Use your napkin often, especially before drinking from a glass. Return it to your lap with the fold toward your knees.

16. Keep your napkin in your lap unless you must excuse yourself temporarily, or until the hostess removes hers from her lap and places it to the left of the place setting signaling that the meal is completed.

17. Never refold a napkin. Simply place it unfolded to the left of your place setting.

18. Never put your napkin on a plate. An exception to this is at a formal dinner, when the napkin may be placed in the center of the clean plate as part of the place setting.

19. Never put used silverware back on the table.

20. If you drop a knife, fork, or spoon, politely ask the hostess for another one. You may pick up a dropped napkin.

Full Place Setting

Simple Place Setting

MANNERS
Made Easy

DINING MANNERS

TEACHING TIP: Don't forget that a mirror is a good teaching tool. Often when we see ourselves perform some of the incorrect ways, we quickly see the reason we should eat correctly.

1. Teach students to label each piece of a full place setting as shown on teacher page 37.

2. Teach students to label each piece of a simple place setting according to the picture (page 37). Notice the open edge of the folded napkin is toward the plate.

3. A dinner napkin is opened halfway and placed in the lap with the fold toward the knees. When the diner picks it up, uses it, and replaces it, the napkin will not leave food stains or smudges on the lap of the diner.

← fold

4. Each utensil should be picked up and held like a pencil, as shown in the illustration.

Continental-style eating is done with the inverted fork in the left hand. The knife remains in the right hand. Both American and Continental ways of eating are correct in our country. (The more common American way is taught here, but if a student has learned to eat Continental style with his or her family, that student should be permitted to continue to do so as long as the fork is inverted in the left hand.) Eating Continental style also permits the diner to place the forearms on the table. In the American style of eating we place the left arm in the lap at all times unless we need to cut the entrée, butter bread, pass something, or use the napkin.

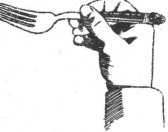

5. Ask each student to demonstrate the correct way to cut their food. Refer to the two illustrations at the bottom of the page. Two additional cutting mistakes to watch for are the "cello method" which draws the elbows up toward one's neighbor, and the "tip of the fork" or "dainty" method in which the diner tries to hold the fork by the tip of the handle with just the thumb and two fingertips.

Correct   Incorrect

6. The term *gangplanking* refers to resting the tip of the handle of a utensil on the table with the point of the bowl or tines of the utensil resting on the plate. Only the iced teaspoon may be propped in that fashion to keep tea stains off the tablecloth. It is never proper to gangplank any of the other utensils.

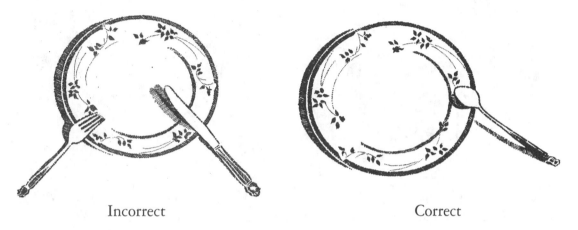

Incorrect   Correct

7. Teach students to place the knife above the fork and spoon in a 10:00 to 4:00 position, making sure the utensils are securely placed on the plate.

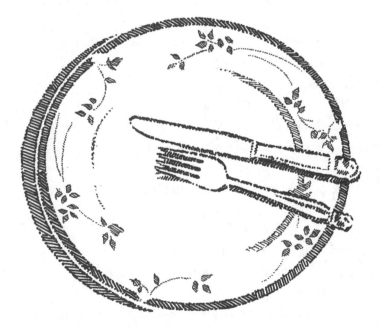

8. Waving and talking with your silverware is dangerous and unpleasant for others to see.
9. Keep your elbows close to your side even while cutting up food.

10. Dip soup away from yourself, gently scraping the bowl of the spoon across the back of the soup bowl to catch any drips.

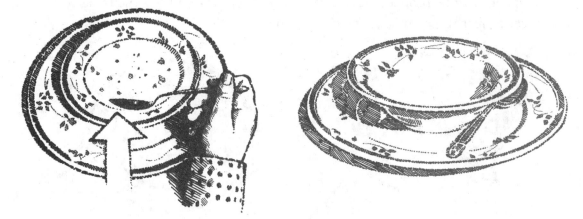

11. The spoon should never be left in the soup bowl during the course or when you finish. Leaving a handle protruding upward from a bowl is dangerous. You might bump the handle and flip the spoon out of the bowl.

12. Place a soup spoon on the service plate beneath the bowl, as shown.

13. Never leave a spoon protruding from a glass. You might poke yourself in the eye. Place the tip of the spoon on the rim of a plate. The back of the spoon should be turned upward.

14. Never touch the rim of a glass or cup with your hands as shown.

15. Slurping drinks is annoying to others.

16. Shoveling food and bending down to meet the plate is impolite and unappetizing to others.

17. Don't scrape your plate clean.

18. Elbows should not be on a table when food is present.

19. Taking food out of your mouth with your hand is unpleasant to all. Cover your mouth with your hand or napkin and remove the food with the utensil you used to put it in your mouth. Then place the unwanted item on your plate, preferably under something like the garnish. If you place it under the rim of your plate and the plate is subsequently removed, you expose the ugly mess.

20. Talking with food in your mouth is most unpleasant for others to see.

21. If you are offered something you cannot eat, simply say "No thank you" or "Thank you, I don't care for any."

22. Taking the last piece of food from a plate or platter is rude.

23. Taking too much food at a time is rude. You should consider how many other people will need to take a serving.

24. Passing food to the right around a table the first time permits diners to take a dish with the left hand, serve themselves with their right hand, and pass it on. After food makes one trip around the table, you may pass it the shortest way to a fellow diner who asks for another serving. (Illustration A)

25. Never use your own utensil to take food from a common dish on the table. If there is not a serving fork or spoon, you may ask the hostess for one.

26. Reaching across the table to get something is rude. You might knock something over. Politely ask someone to pass something to you.

A

27. Licking a bowl, plate, or utensil is unhealthy and unappetizing to others.

28. The salt and pepper should always be passed together even if only one was requested. (Illustration B)

29. Picking one's teeth with a toothpick in public is very unappealing to others.

30. If you have something stuck in your teeth, excuse yourself and take care of the problem in private.

31. Don't say "yuck" at the table.

32. Burping with your mouth open is very rude and unpleasant to others.

B.

33. When a gentleman is seating a lady, she should back up to the chair so that the back of her knees touch the front of the chair. Then she lowers herself straight into the chair. She places her hands on the sides of the chair and helps the gentleman move the chair forward under the table.

MANNERS
Made Easy

LEARNING QUIZ

You may teach the answers as you go through the quiz with the students or you may ask each student to fill in the ones they already know. Another option is to jumble the answers and let the students choose the answers from the list in a multiple-choice fashion. This quiz is for learning, not for testing.

1. What are some of the nice things men and boys can do for ladies? (**Open**) doors and (**help**) ladies with their chairs. The girls should say, (**"Thank you."**)
2. Name some things you should not talk about at the table. (**Gory things, anything argumentative, dieting, etc.**)
3. Do not (**pick**) your teeth at the table or in public.
4. Why do we have table manners? To make everyone's meal (**pleasant; answers will vary.**)
5. Cut (**one**) or two bites of meat at a time. Why? So your food won't look (**messy**) and won't get (**cold**).
6. Is it all right to tilt your chair back? (**No**) Why? (**You might fall or damage the chair**)
7. You should never put your napkin on your (**plate**).
8. What should you do about dental appliances such as retainers? They should be (**taken**) out before you sit down to eat, and put in a pocket or purse.
9. Never talk with (**food**) in your mouth. Never (**point**) with your silverware.
10. What do you say if you don't like something served to you? "I don't (**care**) for any."
11. Why should you dip soup away from you? So you don't (**drip**) it.
12. (**Break**) off one bite at a time from a roll or large piece of bread.
13. Never take the (**last**) piece of (**food**) from a dish or platter.
14. Pass any food or (**condiments**) to the person on your right.
15. Never (**sit**) down until everyone is at the table. Seat the (**ladies**) first.
16. Never leave a (**spoon**) sticking up from a glass or bowl.
17. Start eating with the silverware from the (**outside**) and use the utensils moving inward toward the plate.
18. Boys and men should always (**remove**) their (**hats**) or (**caps**) before entering a building or sitting down to eat. Exception: when you are in a gymnasium.
19. You should always push your (**chair**) back under the table when you get up for any reason.
20. When you finish eating, you should wait until everyone finishes before (**leaving**) the table.
21. Which way should the cutting edge of the knife be turned when you place it on your plate? Toward the (**center**).
22. When you finish eating, place your knife and fork in a (**10:00 to 4:00**) position. Place the (**knife**) above the fork.
23. You should say "yes" or "no" or "yes ma'am" or "no ma'am." What are some things you should not say? (**Yeah, huh, I guess, whatever, etc.**)

24. When you go to a party or to visit, you should always say (**"Hello"**) to the parent or the chaperone as soon as you arrive, and say (**"Thank you**) for inviting me" when you leave.

25. When you are an overnight guest, you should pick up your (**things**) and (**make**) the bed.

26. What should you do if someone says something funny about you? (**Laugh**) or (**ignore**) them.

27. What are some things you should never do to other people? (**Laugh at them about their looks, their name, or their family, gossip about them, make fun of them, etc.**)

28. Is etiquette just a lot of rules to learn or is there a reason for the rules? (**There is a reason.**)

29. What are some reasons for rules of etiquette? (**Consideration for others, safety, to keep from embarrassing oneself or others, etc.**)

 # LESSON SIX BIBLE STUDY

KEY SCRIPTURE REFERENCE:

But when you are invited, go and recline in the lowest place, so that when the one who invited you comes, he will say to you, 'Friend, move up higher.' You will then be honored in the presence of all the other guests. (Luke 14:10)

ADDITIONAL SCRIPTURE REFERENCES:
I Kings 17:7-15, Matt. 6:11, Luke 14:8-14, Luke 22:14-20, and John 21:1-14

BIBLE LESSON:

In the Old Testament, the prophet Elijah asked a widow to prepare a meal for him. When she responded that she had only a cup of flour and bit of oil left, Elijah told her that her obedience would result in an unending supply of flour and oil. She obeyed and never ran out of food again.

In Luke 14, Jesus uses the parable of a great banquet to teach His followers to show kindness and consideration to others. Jesus says that as a guest you should consider that other guests may be more important than you are. In Luke 14:11 He says, *"For everyone who exalts himself will be humbled, and the one who humbles himself will be exalted."*

BIBLE QUIZ

1. Read the story of Elijah and the widow from I Kings 17: 7-15. What lesson can we learn about sharing a meal with others? (**We learn that we will be repaid for showing kindness.**)
2. Write in your own words what Jesus was trying to teach His followers in the parable of the great banquet.
3. Read John 21:1-14 which tells about the meal Jesus prepared for His disciples. How long had the disciples been fishing? (**All night.**)
4. What did Jesus tell them to do when they said they hadn't caught any fish? (**Throw their nets on the right side of the boat.**)
5. Knowing that Jesus was their Savior and Lord, how do you think the disciples felt about Jesus cooking breakfast for them? (**You always feel honored when someone serves a meal to you.**)

MOUTH MANNERS AND OTHER COURTESIES
GENERAL GOOD MANNERS AND COMMON COURTESIES IN A SOCIAL SETTING

1. Never put your feet on the furniture. Keep them on the floor.
2. Never pick at your toes or fingernails in public.
3. Excessive scratching of your head in public is unsanitary.
4. Combing or brushing your hair in public is unsanitary. Excuse yourself to take care of it in private.
5. Picking at your ears is very unpleasant to others.
6. Coughing without covering your mouth is unsanitary and spreads germs. Always cover your mouth, preferably with a tissue.
7. Yawning with your mouth open and uncovered is unpleasant for others.
8. Picking your nose is disgusting to others. It is also unsanitary.
9. Sneezing without covering your mouth is unhealthy. If you are at a dining table, you may use your napkin if you do not have time to reach for a tissue or a handkerchief.
10. Wiping your nose on your arm or sleeve is not sanitary. Excuse yourself, go to the restroom, and blow your nose.
11. Opening a door for someone is kind and helpful.
12. Saying, "I'm sorry" shows concern for others.
13. Laughing at others hurts their feelings.
14. Talking in church or in the movies disturbs others.
15. Gossiping is unkind and hurtful. The gossip is often untrue, but even if you know the topic to be true, it is still wrong to gossip. Think about the Golden Rule.
16. Interrupting is rude. Wait until the person is finished talking on the telephone. If you have an urgent message, you may look them in the eye to get their attention. Then say "Excuse me" before relaying the message.

17. Always push your chair back under a table or desk.
18. Never point or stare at people. Don't walk in front of people. Don't whisper in front of people.
19. Say "Excuse me" anytime you must leave the company of others.

SAYING NO WITHOUT SAYING THANK YOU

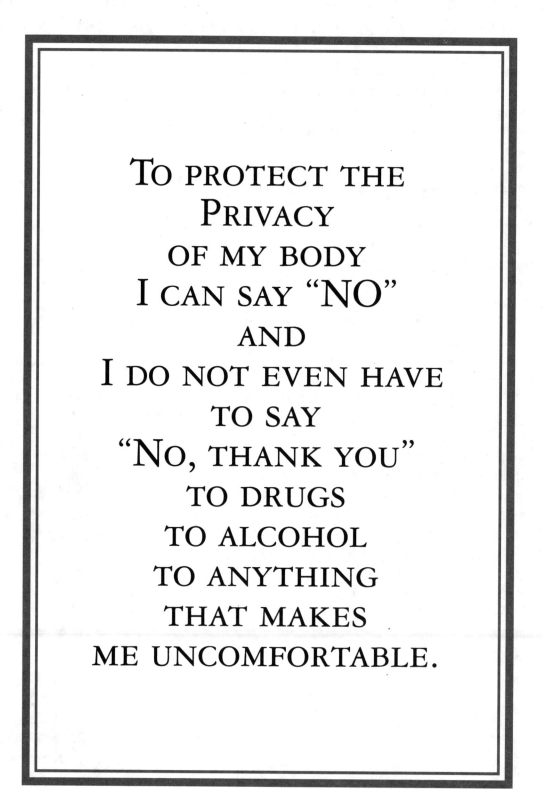

TO PROTECT THE
PRIVACY
OF MY BODY
I CAN SAY "NO"
AND
I DO NOT EVEN HAVE
TO SAY
"NO, THANK YOU"
TO DRUGS
TO ALCOHOL
TO ANYTHING
THAT MAKES
ME UNCOMFORTABLE.

NOTES

NOTES